STUART MCHARDY is a writer, occasional broadcaster and storyteller. Having been actively involved in many aspects of Scottish culture throughout his adult life – music, poetry, language, history, folklore – he has been resident in Edinburgh for over a quarter of a century. Although he has held some illustrious positions, including Director of the Scots Language Resource Centre in Perth and President of the Pictish Arts Society, McHardy is probably proudest of having been a member of the Vigil for a Scottish Parliament. Often to be found in the bookshops, libraries and tea-rooms of Edinburgh, he lives near the city centre with the lovely (and ever-tolerant) Sandra with whom he has one son, Roderick.

DONALD SMITH is the Director of Scottish International Storytelling Festival at Edinburgh's Netherbow and a founder of the National Theatre of Scotland. For many years he was responsible for the programme of the Netherbow Theatre, producing, directing, adapting and writing professional theatre and community dramas, as well as a stream of literature and storytelling events. He has published both poetry and prose, and is a founding member of Edinburgh's Guid Crack Club. He also arranges story walks around Arthur's Seat.

D1337587

Other books by Stuart McHardy:

Scots Poems to be Read Aloud: Yin or Twa Delighfu Evenin's Entertainment (Luath Press, 2001)

The Quest for Arthur (Luath Press, 2001)

The Quest for the Nine Maidens (Luath Press, 2002)

School of the Moon: The Highland Cattle-Raiding Tradition (Birlinn, 2004)

Tales of the Picts (Luath Press, 2005)

On the Trail of the Holy Grail (Luath Press, 2006)

The White Cockade and Other Jacobite Tales (Birlinn, 2006)

Tales of Edinburgh Castle (Luath Press, 2007)

Edinburgh and Leith Pub Guide (Luath Press, 2008)

Tales of Loch Ness (Luath Press, 2009)

Tales of Whisky (Luath Press, 2010)

Speakin o Dundee (Luath Press, 2010)

A New History of the Picts (Luath Press, 2011)

Scotland the Brave Land: 10,000 Years of Scotland in Story (Luath Press, 2012)

Tales of Bonnie Prince Charlie and the Jacobites (Luath Press, 2012)

The Pagan Symbols of the Picts (Luath Press, 2012)

Scotland's Future History (Luath Press, 2015)

Other books by Donald Smith:

John Knox House: Gateway to Edinburgh's Old Town (John Donald Publishers, 1997)

Celtic Travellers: Scotland in the Age of the Saints (Mercat Press, 1997)

Memory Hill (Diehard, 2002)

Storytelling Scotland: A Nation in Narrative (Polygon, 2001)

A Long Stride Shortens the Road: Poems of Scotland (Luath Press, 2004)

Some to Thorns, Some to Thistles (Akros Publications, 2005)

The English Spy (Luath Press, 2007)

God, the Poet and the Devil: Robert Burns and Religion (Saint Andrew Press, 2008)

Between Ourselves (Luath Press, 2013)

Freedom and Faith: A Scottish Question (Saint Andrew Press, 2013)

The Ballad of the Five Marys (Luath Press, 2014)

Pilgrim Guide to Scotland (Saint Andrew Press, 2015)

Other books by Stuart McHardy and Donald Smith:

Arthur's Seat: Journeys and Evocations (Luath Press, 2012)

Calton Hill: Journeys and Evocations (Luath Press, 2013)

Edinburgh Old Town: Journeys and Evocations, with John Fee (Luath Press, 2014)

Scotland's
Democracy Trail

STUART McHARDY and DONALD SMITH

Luath Press Limited
EDINBURGH
www.luath.co.uk

First published 2015

ISBN: 978-1-910021-67-5

The paper used in this book is recyclable. It is made from low
chlorine pulps produced in a low energy, low emissions manner
from renewable forests.

Map by Mike Fox

Photographs by Stuart McHardy unless otherwise stated

'Freedom Come-All-Ye' reproduced by kind permission
of Kätzel Henderson

Typeset in 11 point Sabon by
3btype.com

Printed and bound by
The Charlesworth Group, Wakefield

*Dedicated to all those
who have struggled for Scotland*

▲ View of the beginning of the trail, taken from Arthur's Seat

Courtesy of Ad Meskens, Wikimedia Commons

Contents

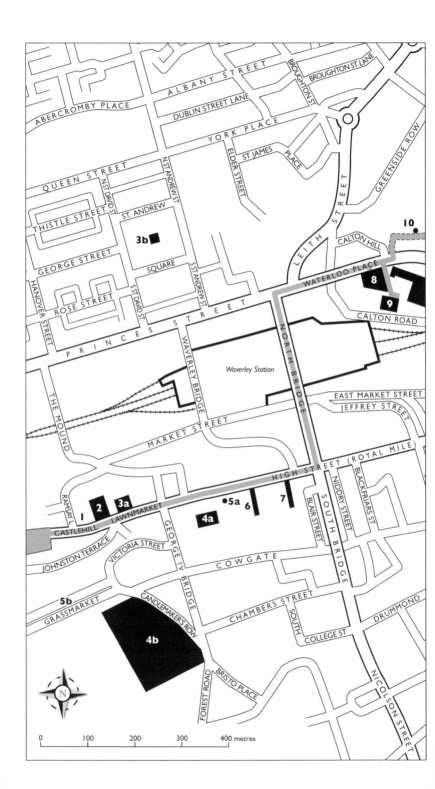

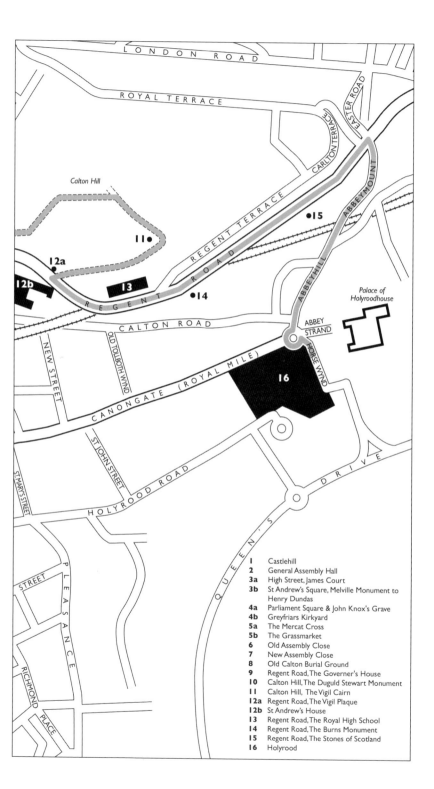

1   Castlehill
2   General Assembly Hall
3a High Street, James Court
3b St Andrew's Square, Melville Monument to
    Henry Dundas
4a Parliament Square & John Knox's Grave
4b Greyfriars Kirkyard
5a The Mercat Cross
5b The Grassmarket
6   Old Assembly Close
7   New Assembly Close
8   Old Calton Burial Ground
9   Regent Road, The Governer's House
10 Calton Hill, The Duguld Stewart Monument
11 Calton Hill, The Vigil Cairn
12a Regent Road, The Vigil Plaque
12b St Andrew's House
13 Regent Road, The Royal High School
14 Regent Road, The Burns Monument
15 Regent Road, The Stones of Scotland
16 Holyrood

▲ Entrance to Edinburgh Castle

Courtesy of Chris Sherlock, Wikimedia Commons

Introduction

SCOTLAND'S DEMOCRACY TRAIL goes from Edinburgh Castle, down the High Street, across North Bridge to Calton Hill, and then on to the Scottish Parliament at Holyrood. Apart from its historic significance, the route encompasses Edinburgh's most dramatic scenery and townscape.

The Trail follows the emergence of democratic thought and action in Scotland from the 16th century, linking pivotal events to locations on the way. It is a story of ups and downs, triumphs and tragedies, borne along by a stubborn, persistent advance.

The Trail moves back and forward in time showing the connections between influential ideas and key personalities in different periods. The roots of democracy run deep in Scotland – the leader of the Caledonians at the Battle of Mons Graupius in c. 80CE was said by Tacitus to have talked of 'Freedom'.

The pervasive influence of the 1320 Declaration of Arbroath must be acknowledged here, but our Trail concentrates on the footprint of democracy in our capital city. Attention is drawn to the roles of America and France in developing 18th century Scottish calls for parliamentary reform, but it is worth remembering that there were also Scots involved in the American Revolution, drawing on already established traditions of democratic thought.

As far back as the early 16th century, John Mair, a Scottish philosopher famed throughout Europe, postulated, among other things, that the people of a nation were more important than its kings, and that even non-Christian 'savages' had rights. Half a century later George Buchanan, after travelling extensively though Europe, became a Protestant and took the position of tutor to the young James VI. In his 1579 *De Jure Regni apud Scotos* (a dialogue concerning the due privilege of government in the kingdom of Scotland) he insisted that kings were not above the law. This was greatly influential in Scottish and British Protestant thinking.

To help make things clearer there is a timeline at the back of the book which gives a general historical background and then specific Scottish milestones.

The idea of *Scotland's Democracy Trail* was suggested to the authors by the Minister for Culture and External Affairs, Fiona Hyslop MSP, on a visit to the Scottish Storytelling Centre with the Greek Ambassador to the United Kingdom in February 2014.

Stuart McHardy and Donald Smith
Edinburgh, June 2014

Looking down the Royal Mile ▶

CHAPTER ONE

Castlehill

Map Location 1

STAND BESIDE THE narrow built-up passage that connects the town of Edinburgh to the fortress and Royal Palace of Edinburgh Castle. You can see today's tourists crowding up into the approach. Historically this was a passageway of power. At the upper end, in Scotland's premier stronghold and prison were sited royal sovereignty backed by military muscle, patronage through land and honours, a judicial right of life or death, and taxation, however inefficient. Below were the landowners with their townhouses and court offices, the merchants, the burgh citizens and the common people.

In medieval times and into the early modern period, hierarchy was the order of the day with the monarchy at the top of the pyramid. Only God ranked higher, though his earthly representatives in the Church struggled to influence 'disobedient' kings and queens who felt they had their own hotline to divine legitimacy. The monarchs would descend in procession down Castlehill to display their authority and wealth for all to behold and acknowledge. Sometimes their power was demonstrated by pageants, sometimes through imprisonments, executions and other ritual humiliations, all designed to overawe and entertain the mob.

Yet even in the medieval period the power of hierarchy was limited by obligations and duties that went up and down the scale. Rulers were bound into a contract with the ruled. Failure to play their part could lead to overthrow or worse. In practice most medieval monarchs struggled to exercise effective authority and desperately needed loyalty and practical support from those below to deliver on their appointed functions. In Scotland central government was perpetually short of cash and depended on financial contributions from churchmen, aristocrats (normally extracted under threat of confiscation) and the burgh merchants. Moreover, as Scotland had no standing army, defence against enemies within or without crucially required the willingness of the earls, knights and chiefs to muster in the cause.

One famous early incident illustrates this vividly. When struggling to retain their independence from England in the early 14th century, the Scots deposed King John Balliol, who had been selected by Edward I of England and came to be seen as his weak puppet, 'Toom Tabard' (meaning 'empty coat'). Far from unanimously, the Scots crowned Robert Bruce in Balliol's place, but his descendants refused to accept the legitimacy of this deposition, sustaining an intermittent civil war, with English support, for another 50 years.

In light of these events, the Community of the Realm of Scotland, composing of the Three Estates of Lords, Bishops and Burgh merchants, asserted in the 1320 Declaration of Arbroath that kingship in the realm of Scotland was conditional on the monarch performing his or her duties. Should Robert Bruce himself fail to deliver, the Declaration asserts, then he too would be replaced.

> Unto him, as the man through whom salvation has been wrought in our people, we are bound both of right and by his service rendered, and are resolved in whatever fortune to cleave, for the preservation of our liberty. Were he to abandon the enterprise begun, choosing to subject us or our kingdom to the king of the English or to the English people, we would strive to thrust him out forthwith as our enemy and the subverter of right, his own and ours, and take for our king another who would suffice for our defence; for so long as an hundred remain alive we are minded never a whit to bow beneath the yoke of English dominion. It is not for glory, riches or honours that we fight: it is for liberty alone, the liberty which no good man relinquishes but with is life.

Royal succession might give you access to the throne but it did not guarantee keeping it. In England the earlier Magna Carta of 1215, which was imposed on a reluctant and unpopular King John, is a similar expression of 'contractual kingship'. It was not until the 17th century that the idea of 'absolute kingship' developed in royalist opposition to more radical ideas about the rights of subjects or citizens. The medieval Stewart kings of Scotland swore a coronation oath that contained this pledge:

> I shall be real and true to God and Haly Kirk and to the Thrie Estaitis of my realm. And ilk estait keep, defend, and govern in their ain freedom and privilege, at my guidlie power, after the laws and customs of the realm… and nothing to work na use touching the common profit of the realm without consent of the Thrie Estaitis.

One episode in this Castlehill location concerns the imprisonment in Edinburgh Castle of James III by his over-mighty aristocratic subjects. In fact Scots kings were frequently held hostage by lordly factions who could combine their armed followings to seize power by force. This happened especially when the ruler was a minor and each faction sought control over the Royal Court and its powers. In this instance

▼ The General Assembly Hall, as seen from the Mound
Courtesy of Rep0n1x, Wikimedia Commons

however in 1482, the people of Edinburgh rose up to free the King from his captors. In response James granted the citizens a 'Golden Charter' enshrining their right to take up arms in defence of their freedoms and privileges.

Tradition connects this lost 'Charter' with 'The Blue Blanket', a banner belonging to the Trades or Craft Guilds, which hung in the Chapel of St Eloi in St Giles' Cathedral. This chapel, which survives in today's cathedral without its earlier adornments, was maintained by the Guild of Hammermen or metalworkers, and their later offshoot, the Goldsmiths. Legend ascribes the original making of the Blue Blanket to the Crusades, but its likely origin is 1482. In 1513 it was carried at the Battle of Flodden from where it returned, despite the loss of Scottish life at that tragic defeat. Later the Blanket became a symbol of the Covenanters' right to bear arms in their own religious and political crusade.

A 17th century version of the Blue Blanket survives in the care of the Convenery of the Trades of Edinburgh. In the 1980s a reproduction of this banner featured as the centrepiece of an Old Town community drama, and it was carried in the Edinburgh's May Day procession once again in 2014. The inscription reads:

> Fear God and honour the King with a long lyffe and prosperous reign and we that are Trades shall ever pray to be faithful for the defence of his sacred Majesty's royal person till death.

In these earlier centuries Scottish kingship was not radically different from the European norms. But Scots rulers lived close to their subjects and could only reign effectively with a degree of popular consent and support. This was expressed through the Three Estates of the Lords, the Church and the burghs which were represented mainly by the merchants. It was also the fact that the kings of Scots spoke the same language, Scots, as the rest of the population.

In more remote regions, the earls and lords were effectively rulers in their own right. But people in the lowlands and burghs who saw the monarchs going about their business were loyal to Royal Government, on condition that it was exercised for the wellbeing, or commonweal, of the nation as a whole. Rulers were titled King or Queen of Scots rather than Scotland, emphasising the nature of this two-way relationship between monarch and people.

General Assembly Building, High Street　▶

CHAPTER TWO

General Assembly Hall

Map Location 2

POLITICAL CHANGE IN Scotland came in some unexpected guises. Sir David Lyndsay was the Lyon Herald at the Court of James v, whom he tutored as a bereaved youngster after James iv's death at Flodden. Lyndsay was a landowner at the heart of the Scottish establishment. Yet Lyndsay also wrote and produced a medieval morality play which, like 7:84 Theatre in the 20th century, has biting political edge. *Ane Satyre of the Thrie Estaitis* demanded

social reform, and root and branch reorganisation of the church hierarchy, while stopping short of advocating the Protestantism that was active across northern Europe in the 16th century.

All the authorities of the day, including the King, are confronted in the play by John Commonweal who leaps over the barrier into the assembly to demand justice on behalf of the poor and oppressed. It is a dramatic coup and a vivid moment of challenge to all established order. 'Reform or else', seems to be Lyndsay's prophetic warning, though he sweetens the pill with a riotous farcical ending that throws everything back in the faces of the audience, 'fools all'. Here is John at his point of maximum impact:

> JOHN:
> Out of my gait! For God's sake let me gae!
> Tell me, gude maister, again whit ye say.
>
> DILIGENCE:
> I warn all that be wrongously offendit,
> Come and complain and they sall be amendit…
> What is they name, fellow? That wad I feil.
>
> JOHN:
> Forsooth they call me John the Common-Weal.
> Gude maister, I wad speir at you ane thing-
> Where traist ye sall I find yon new-made King?
>
> DILIGENCE:
> Come over and I will show thee to his grace.
>
> JOHN:
> God's benison licht in that lucky face!
> Stand by the gait; let see if I can loup.
> I maun rin fast, in case I gat ane coup
> (Heir sall John loup the ditch, or fall in it)
>
> KING:
> Show me thy name, gude man, I thee command.

JOHN:
Marry, John the Common-Weal of fair Scotland.

KING: (looking at John's rags)
The Common-Weal has been amang his faes.

JOHN:
Yea, Sir. That gars the Common-Weal want claes!

KING:
What is the cause the Common-Weal is cruikit?

JOHN:
Because the Common-Weal has been overlukit.

KING:
What gars thee look sae with ane dreary heart?

JOHN:
Because the Thrie Estaitis gangs all backwart.

This superb theatrical epic was revived in 1948 at the second Edinburgh International Festival in the Church of Scotland General Assembly Hall, which has the advantage of being designed as both a court and parliament for the Presbyterian Church. The production by Tyrone Guthrie was also the first use of a Shakespearean style thrust stage in modern theatre. The version of the play used was a much shortened adaptation by Robert Kemp, which skilfully focuses on the more conventional morality play structures. It was not until 2013 that a complete five-hour version of *The Thrie Estaitis* was staged, outdoors at Linlithgow, restoring the hard-edged politics, the exuberant bawdiness and the full blast of the rumbustious finale.

Lyndsay lived to witness the first attempt at Protestant Reformation in Scotland, which ended at St Andrews with the capture of the castle by French forces in 1548, and the removal of a young priest-turned-preacher John Knox to serve time as a galley slave. In 1559 Knox returned from exile at the behest of a powerful faction of the Scots nobility, some of whom were Protestant by conviction, but all of whom coveted a share of royal power and the old Church's wealth. Within a generation John Commonweal had become Knox the Reformer with much more radical consequences.

John Knox was first and foremost a religious reformer. His thinking was based on the position that everything you needed to know about religion was in the Bible, and that the Holy Spirit would tell you what it meant rather than the hierarchy of the Church which had corrupted the pure 'Word of God'. Nonetheless the Church remained important for Knox as its job was to preach 'God's Word' and guide everyone on the right path, not least rulers and magistrates.

Knox was not one of Protestantism's original theologians, but he pushed its political and social implications further than most, with lasting consequences in Scotland. Knox's line was that if a 'tyrannous' ruler oppressed true religion and imposed unjust or immoral laws, then such laws could be disobeyed and the ruler overthrown, if necessary. In such circumstances violence might be justified. This line challenges the central tenets of European society at the time – the legitimacy of royal rule, the religious obligation to obey the authorities, and social order sustained by religion and law working together.

Many of Knox's aristocratic Protestant allies in Scotland had no intention of upturning the social order; they wanted control of it for themselves. In addition many fellow reformers, including Knox's mentor John Calvin, were not prepared to preach Knox's version of civil disobedience. Establishment Protestants such as Mathew Parker, the Archbishop of Canterbury were horrified, claiming that if Knox had his way 'no master might sleep safe in his bed'. Yet Knox is the ancestor of generations of radical religious dissenters, and of all those in modern times who have disobeyed oppressive laws in the name of conscience. Paradoxically of course, Knox's position is based not on liberty but on obedience to his version of 'God's Word'.

A man with Knox's views was never going to exist comfortably with Scottish political realities, and so it proved. He was bitterly disappointed that the Three Estates in Parliament – dominated by the nobility – refused to implement his agenda for radical social reform, including education and social security. When Mary Queen of Scots returned from France in 1561, Knox was convinced that she was aiming to restore Roman Catholicism, and his attacks on her became increasingly outspoken and angry as his fears mounted.

A particular bugbear for Knox was the young widowed Queen's marriage, and the danger that she would make a Catholic alliance which would return Scotland to the European fold, so undermining the Protestant alliance with England. Now Minster of St Giles' Cathedral in Edinburgh, Knox whipped up opposition to a Catholic marriage, and a furious Mary summoned him to the palace at Holyrood. Marriage and succession were a matter of royal prerogative, central to the exercise and status of hierarchical power. What did a mere preacher have to do with it? Knox leaves us this vivid account of the exchange, which is worthy of Lyndsay's dramatic talents.

> MARY:
> What have you to do with my marriage?

> KNOX:
> If it please your Majesty to hear me patiently, I shall show the truth in plain words. I grant that your Grace has offered me more courtesy and kindness than I ever required; but God did not send me to wait upon the Courts of Princesses or in ladies' chambers, I am sent to preach the Evangel of Jesus Christ to such as please to hear it... The magic of your Person, Madam, has so worked upon the Nobility that they heed neither God His Word nor yet their duty to the Commonwealth. It becomes me to remind them of these things.

> MARY:
> I ask you again, what have you to do with my marriage? What are you within this Commonwealth?

> KNOX:
> A subject born within the same. I am neither Earl, Lord nor Baron, and to your eyes I may appear of small account. But both my vocation and my conscience crave plainness of me. And therefore, Madam, to yourself I say that which I speak in a public place: whensoever the Nobility of this Realm shall consent that you be subject to an unfaithful and renegade husband, on that day they shall do as much as lies in them to renounce Christ, to banish His truth, to betray the freedom of the Realm and, perhaps, in the end, to do small comfort to yourself.

As it turned out, Mary made her choice of a royal marriage to her Stewart cousin Henry Darnley. Like Mary, he had a place in the English royal succession through their shared grandmother Margaret Tudor, and he was at least nominally Catholic. The marriage was a disaster for Mary and Scotland, though not for reasons of religion.

In the course of his disputes with a series of Catholic queens including Mary's mother, Marie de Guise, John Knox deploys the patriarchal prejudices of his day against female rulers. These come out in his arguments against Mary's marriage, since unlike her, he imagines her royal husband as assuming the reins of government. In fact Mary was determined to be Queen in every sense. Knox's sexism seems inconsistent with his general principles of equality before God, and with his personal attitude to friends and spouses. These politicised attacks on women rulers – 'the monstrous regiment (rule) of women' – remain a stain on Knox's achievements to this day.

What is more interesting in Knox's dialogue is the emerging concept of citizenship. A Christian for Knox is part of a 'Godly Commonwealth' and this involves influencing civil society as well as the Church, since both are subject to 'God's Word'. Moreover members of this commonwealth should be educated to read and understand the Bible for themselves. This in turn involves training teachers and ministers in languages, rhetoric, philosophy and logic, history, theology and mathematics. Education becomes the basis of reform across all aspects of corporate and personal life.

So the groundwork is laid for eventual universal education, critical thought, democratic citizenship and the Scottish Enlightenment. Of course medieval Catholic education espoused many of the same objectives, which was why the reform process was not a total break with the past. But the medieval church was also a pillar of hierarchy, while Knox's vision was already universal in potential, even though it was founded on a more divisive view of religion. His very argumentative determination to separate 'the sheep from the goats' became a stimulus to critical questioning and thought.

Education was to be the driver for future social and political change. In addition, printing could now provide texts for an increasingly literate public. People could read the words and then argue about what they meant, privately and publicly. The French novelist Victor Hugo observed that printing turned the Protestant movement from just another schism of the Church into a revolution. However, as Knox died in 1572, possibly in the Edinburgh house that still bears his name, centuries of struggle and dispute lay ahead in both church and state.

As we stand here at the head of the Royal Mile, we are surrounded by three General Assembly Halls. The current Church of Scotland Assembly Hall, which housed Lyndsay's *Satyre* in 1948 and the reconvened Scottish Parliament in 1999, was built by the Free Church of Scotland. It broke away en masse from the national Kirk in the 1843 Disruption, in protest at State interference in matters such as the appointment of ministers to parishes. The present day Edinburgh International Festival Hub, with its spire by Pugin, was the Assembly Hall of the Established or 'Auld Kirk' of Scotland, which reunited with most of the Free Church in 1929. However as the various Presbyterian Churches reunited, minorities objected, so creating continuing separate denominations such as the present day Free Church whose General Assembly meets in St Columba's Free Church on the opposite side of the road from the present day Church of Scotland Assembly. Just a little further along is St Columba's

by the Castle Episcopal Church, but its existence concerns another political hot potato which we will handle at a later location.

▲ Statue of John Knox, outside the Assembly Hall on the Mound

Courtesy of Kim Traynor, Wikimedia Commons

CHAPTER THREE

High Street, James Court

Map Location 3a

COMING OFF THE Royal Mile into this quiet courtyard we enter a different world, and period. In 1727 James Court was a new development of four tenement blocks arranged around a square, built by James Brownhill. Each house was contained on one floor, and designed to be identical to those above and below. This was a new style of design, which made buildings much cheaper and easier to construct.

The flats in James Court were more spacious, lighter and airier than traditional tenements, and therefore more expensive. Brownhill held parties and balls to attract potential dwellers. In the beginning James Court was the home of professionals, merchants and gentry. Over the years many well-known people lived in the square, including the philosopher and historian David Hume and author James Boswell. Here we see what was later called 'the Scottish Enlightenment' taking shape in the Old Town before the move to Edinburgh's classically ordered New Town.

It was here in Lawrie's Rooms that the 1792 Convention of the Societies of the Friends of the

◀ James Court

People was held. This Convention was held to call for democratic reform, something the then Prime Minister William Pitt had earlier supported, in opposition. The Convention brought people from all walks of life from all over Scotland and had visiting members from brother societies in England and Ireland. It was noteworthy that the membership fees of the Scottish societies were set at a level where working men could join, unlike those in England which effectively restricted membership to the gentry. This is perhaps a reflection of the much wider level of literacy in Scotland than elsewhere at the time, meaning that the works of writers such as Thomas Paine were more likely to be read amongst the ordinary people here. This of course could only further feed the paranoia of a ruling elite that saw itself under imminent threat from the ideas of the French Revolution.

As in England and Ireland the idea of such societies was to try and put pressure on the government to reform the parliamentary system which was endemically corrupt. Not only was there an incredibly limited electorate, but the buying and selling of parliamentary seats was an almost everyday occurrence. With the breakaway of the American colonies and their revolutionary slogan, 'no taxation without representation', and then the upheaval of the French revolution with its slogan 'Liberty, Equality, Fraternity', the need for reforming the corrupt system of British parliamentary government had never been so clear. The works of Englishman Thomas Paine, *The Age of Reason* and *The Rights of Man* were selling in tens of thousands across Britain.

While the British Prime Minister William Pitt had been amongst those calling for reform in the 1780s, now that he was in power, like many a politician before and since, he changed his tune. Why mess with a system that was serving him and his friends so well?

Nowhere was the corruption greater than in Scotland. Scotland's MPs were a pathetic irrelevance and all power was in the hands of one man, Henry Dundas, Viscount Melville (Map Location 3b – the Melville Monument). He was a member of *Pitt's* Cabinet, rising to the position of First Lord of the Admiralty at the same time as running Scotland as a virtual one-man dictatorship, until he was forced to resign amid widespread accusations of corruption in 1805. Up till then he had absolute control over all government patronage in Scotland, which he used to enrich himself and further the interests of his family. He was so powerful that he was given the nickname King Harry the Ninth.

Many of the British ruling class at the time had initially welcomed the French Revolution, thinking that the revolutionaries were going to create something like the British system of government with its much vaunted partnership between monarch and people. When it began to look like the French were intent on creating a real democracy, that attitude changed. When the French revolutionaries had the temerity to execute their king, Louis XVI – after being tried for treason due to his plotting with foreign powers to overthrow the revolutionary Government of France – Britain declared war on France. The Societies of Friends of the People were deemed to be no better than the French revolutionaries and were seen as trying to overthrow the whole system of British governance, which those who controlled it claimed was the finest and fairest in the history of the world. The fact that the reformers, generally referred to as Radicals, repeatedly insisted that they had no intention of overthrowing the government and went out of their way to declare the commitment to peaceful means meant nothing to Dundas and those who flourished under his protection.

Here in James Court the reforming radicals laid out their ideas and the widespread support for their programme can be seen in the support they had from Robert Burns, which is discussed below. These reformers advocated greater freedom so that human beings could improve individually and socially. They saw a direct link between morality and politics, and between freedom and knowledge.

Some of the attendees at the Convention did think that the lawyer Thomas Muir in particular was a bit too radical, but time and again it was stated that the intention of the Convention wanted to peaceably reform the current system through parliamentary means. From the point of view of the Establishment however even this moderate challenge to the status quo was blatant sedition. Reaction to the calls for reform was brutal and several of the leading members like Thomas Muir and Fyshe Palmer, a preacher, were transported for sedition to Botany Bay after disgracefully partisan show trials.

It is a touch ironic that today James Court is the location of a fine basement pub called The Jolly Judge. The judge who presided over the trial of Muir and his friends, Lord Braxfield, was anything but jolly. At the trial of another Radical, George Mealmaker, charged with sedition for distributing the works of Thomas Paine, the defendant drew a comparison between what he and his fellows were trying to achieve and Jesus Christ's cleansing of the moneylenders from the temple. Braxfield growled, in his native Scots, 'Muckle guid it did him, he wis hangit tae!' which translates as 'A lot of good that did him, he was hanged too!' This was a perfect example of the judicial impartiality to be expected under Henry Dundas' brutal rule.

Amongst those who attended the Convention were delegates from England and Ireland, and the latter in particular were seen as a particular problem

▼ The Jolly Judge, James Court

by the powers that be. Unlike Scotland, which was one of the constituent nations of the United Kingdom of Great Britain and Ireland, Ireland had in fact been conquered by England and absorbed under direct rule. Effectively Scotland under Dundas was treated in no less colonial a fashion, but legally and constitutionally Scotland has always been accorded its own national status, at least on paper. In Ireland there was always an undercurrent of agitation for independence and it is of significant interest that even back then Protestants as well as Catholics were involved in the search for reform. The language of the message from the Irish convention hints at something more than simple reform but time and again the delegates stressed their commitment to working through parliamentary procedures to achieve change.

St Giles' Cathedral ▶

CHAPTER FOUR

Parliament Square and John Knox's Grave

Map Location 4a

WE ARE HIDDEN quietly behind the bulk of St Giles'
Cathedral, and surrounded by Scotland's High
Courts. Concealed amidst them is Parliament Hall
where, in 1707, the Scottish Parliament approved
the Union with England and so with it its own
abolition. We are also standing on what was the
graveyard where John Knox was supposedly buried.

The figure dominating the Square and kitted out as Julius Caesar astride his bronze horse in formal triumph, is Charles I during whose reign Parliament Hall was built. Charles was also the catalyst for Scotland's period of civil and religious strife in the 17th century, ensuring this small northern nation a full share in Europe's long-drawn-out Wars of Religion.

It is not, however, fair to pin all the blame on Charles I or on a London Government, though from 1603 Royal Government was centred in London following James VI of Scotland's succession as James I of Great Britain and Ireland. The trouble began much earlier as Scottish Government tried to rein

▲ Parliament Square

THE ABOVE STONE
MARKS THE APPROXIMATE
SITE OF THE BURIAL
IN ST GILES GRAVEYARD
- OF JOHN KNOX -
THE GREAT SCOTTISH DIVINE
WHO DIED 24 NOV 1572

back radical Presbyterianism. Even the pious Regent
Moray had fallen out with Knox and his demands,
and a few years later the much less pious Regent
Morton made the first steps towards restoring
royally appointed Bishops as a counterweight to the
preachers.

James VI was peaceful and ecumenical in matters
of religion, but also keen to restore a royal
prerogative. So he insisted on Episcopal governance
of the Presbyterian Church. He also expatiated on
the divine right of kings and he instilled that belief
into his young sons Henry and then Charles. As a
child James had been beaten and lectured by the
dourly republican though intellectually brilliant

▲ Site of John Knox's grave, Parliament Square

George Buchanan, and he was determined never to see royalty subjected to such treatment again. Charles learnt his father's lesson all too well, adding high religious beliefs to his absolutist politics.

Charles' approach was combustible in England but positively explosive in Scotland. He attempted to impose an English Prayer Book on the Scots Kirk, so reviving all the earlier religious controversies while igniting national resentment towards distant and autocratic political rule from London. On the first day a service was to be read from the new book here in St Giles. A riot ensued, provoked by Jenny Geddes hurling her stool at the pulpit and reputedly crying, 'Dare ye say Mass in my lug (ear)'. Populist anti-Catholicism was now strongly embedded in most Lowland towns, denouncing any flavour of liturgy, vestments or adornment as 'papist'.

More significantly, a vigorous movement for national reassertion ensued, leading to the signing of the National Covenant in 1638 in Greyfriars Kirkyard. You can visit the site close by, past the National Library on George IV Bridge (Map Location 4b). Greyfriars Kirk also contains interpretations and displays about these dramatic events.

The National Covenant however was not a religious revolution, but a dignified and detailed constitutional affirmation of all the legal and ecclesiastical structures of Scotland over which Charles I was riding roughshod. The concept of Covenant is taken from Judaeo-Christian thought, originally meaning a bond or mutual promise between God and his chosen people. In the Scottish sense the bond, or 'band' as it was referred to in Scots, implied the first meaning but also a resolve

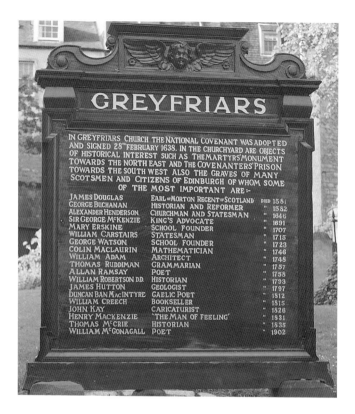

GREYFRIARS

IN GREYFRIARS CHURCH THE NATIONAL COVENANT WAS ADOPTED AND SIGNED 28TH FEBRUARY 1638. IN THE CHURCHYARD ARE OBJECTS OF HISTORICAL INTEREST SUCH AS THE MARTYRS' MONUMENT TOWARDS THE NORTH EAST AND THE COVENANTERS' PRISON TOWARDS THE SOUTH WEST ALSO THE GRAVES OF MANY SCOTSMEN AND CITIZENS OF EDINBURGH OF WHOM SOME OF THE MOST IMPORTANT ARE:-

		DIED	
JAMES DOUGLAS	EARL OF MORTON REGENT OF SCOTLAND	DIED	1581
GEORGE BUCHANAN	HISTORIAN AND REFORMER	"	1582
ALEXANDER HENDERSON	CHURCHMAN AND STATESMAN	"	1646
SIR GEORGE M°KENZIE	KING'S ADVOCATE	"	1691
MARY ERSKINE	SCHOOL FOUNDER	"	1707
WILLIAM CARSTAIRS	STATESMAN	"	1715
GEORGE WATSON	SCHOOL FOUNDER	"	1723
COLIN MACLAURIN	MATHEMATICIAN	"	1746
WILLIAM ADAM	ARCHITECT	"	1748
THOMAS RUDDIMAN	GRAMMARIAN	"	1757
ALLAN RAMSAY	POET	"	1758
WILLIAM ROBERTSON D.D.	HISTORIAN	"	1793
JAMES HUTTON	GEOLOGIST	"	1797
DUNCAN BAN M°INTYRE	GAELIC POET	"	1812
WILLIAM CREECH	BOOKSELLER	"	1815
JOHN KAY	CARICATURIST	"	1826
HENRY MACKENZIE	"THE MAN OF FEELING"	"	1831
THOMAS M°CRIE	HISTORIAN	"	1835
WILLIAM M°GONAGALL	POET	"	1902

that all those who signed would band together in defence of the Covenant's principles. Many moderates including the distinguished Marquis of Montrose signed the National Covenant:

> That all Kings and Princes at their Coronation and reception of their Princely Authority, shall make their faithful promise by their solemn oath in the presence of the Eternal God to the uttermost of their power, according as He hath required in his most Holy Word, contained in the Old and New Testament. And according the same Word will maintain the true Religion of Christ... and shall rule the people committed to their charge, according to the will and

▲ Covenanters Memorial, Greyfriars Kirkyard

command of God, revealed in his foresaid Word, and according to the laudable Laws and Constitutions received in this Realm, no ways repugnant to the said will of the Eternal God; and shall procure, to the uttermost of their power, to the Kirk of God and whole Christian people, true and perfect peace in all time coming.

Unfortunately the political crisis deepened and civil war broke out across the Three Kingdoms of England, Scotland and Ireland. At stake were the intertwined issues of religious authority and its relationship to civil government and the monarchy. In 1643 the National Covenant was superseded for devout Presbyterians by the Solemn League and Covenant. It was a much stronger religious statement of the need for church and state to conform to reformed Protestantism, verging on theocracy. This was a step too far for many Scots, including Montrose who switched to the royalist side. The outcomes were bloody for all, not least Charles I and the gallant Marquis, both of whom were executed.

Here in St Giles' Cathedral we can see the tombs of both Montrose and his great enemy the Covenanting Marquis of Argyll, who was executed in turn following the fall of the Puritan Commonwealth and the restoration of Charles II. It is worth noting that Oliver Cromwell's short-lived commonwealth abolished Scotland as an independent nation by force of arms, something that even Edward I, 'Hammer of the Scots', failed to achieve.

However on the restoration of the monarchy, the Scots Parliament was also restored and continued with an increasing role until the 1707 Union. The disputes between Episcopal and Presbyterian church systems also continued, with the latter finally

coming out on top following the overthrow of James II and VII and the installation of William of Orange as King in 1689. Securing a Protestant succession, which led to the Union of the Crowns in 1603, was also the principal motive behind the Incorporating Parliamentary Union of 1707, which prevented a Scottish Parliament going in a different direction from London and reversing the 1603 Union of the Crowns. James' deposition and exile sparked the Jacobite movement and led to successive attempts at restoration, principally in Scotland.

Parliament Hall is a magnificent parliament chamber, and worth visiting before we pay our respects to the executed leaders in St Giles.

▲ Parliament Hall, Parliament Square
Courtesy of Kim Traynor, Wikimedia Commons

CHAPTER FIVE

The Mercat Cross

Map Location 5a

THIS IS THE ceremonial centre of civic Edinburgh. The magnificent 'Riding of the Parliament' would wend its way past here to Old Parliament Hall. Proclamations and edicts were pronounced here by heralds, and important news spread out from into the taverns, change houses and later coffee houses. On occasions of royal pageantry, much rarer after 1603, wine would flow like water at the Mercat Cross to please the crowd.

More soberly, the merchants gathered by the Cross to exchange trade intelligence and discuss deals. The city's intellectuals were also in the mix, meeting and greeting, before repairing to the bookshops, printers, and their own convivial gatherings, which fuelled the ongoing Scottish Enlightenment, cutting across specialisms in a general quest for human understanding. This makes it a good place to site Alexander Stoddart's contemporary statue of Adam Smith, author of *The Theory of Moral Sentiments* and *The Wealth of Nations*, in that order.

But the Mercat Cross was also the focal point for protest and riots. Edinburgh was notorious for the

◄ The Mercat Cross

Courtesy of Kim Traynor, Wikimedia Commons

readiness of its 'mob' to rise up in angry demonstrations. The structure of the town lends itself to assembling a crowd which can quickly impact on the life and mood of the city. The closeness of all the authorities – civic, legal and ecclesiastical – adds point to the protest and the town jail, Edinburgh's Tolbooth, was conveniently located near the west end of St Giles if someone needed to be broken out of their imprisonment.

With an electoral system that effectively disbarred over 95 per cent of the population from participation in decisions that directly affected their own lives, the people in the cities had only one real weapon with which to express their dissent or

▲ The Mercat Cross, High Street

SCOTLAND'S DEMOCRACY TRAIL

dissatisfaction with the actions of their rulers – riot. The Edinburgh Mob in particular was renowned throughout Europe. This was partially due to an event in 1736 which has gone down in history as The Porteous Riot.

Andrew Wilson, a convicted smuggler, was publicly hanged on 14 April 1736 in the Grassmarket (Map Location 5b). Although Wilson had been convicted of robbing the Pittenweem customs house in Fife, the general population felt a great deal of sympathy towards him. This was down to the fact that increased taxes on alcohol had led to widespread smuggling. At the time smuggling referred not only to the importation of foreign alcohol but the making of it in Scotland when duty was avoided. In subsequent years the 'peatreek' industry, which was the term for illegally distilled whisky, became a cornerstone of the rural economy. Public sympathy was always with the smugglers and against the excisemen or gaugers who attempted to control or eradicate the peatreek industry and the importing of foreign drink. In addition to this Wilson was seen as a bit of a hero as he had helped co-accused George Robertson to escape from open court, effectively sacrificing himself to ensure his friend's freedom. Robertson's escape had been further helped by the public preventing the various officers of the law from pursuing him.

The crowd at the hanging were unhappy at Wilson's execution and as feelings rose stones were thrown at the members of the Town Guard, commanded by Captain John Porteous. Porteous gave the guard the order to fire directly into the crowd and several people were killed, most of them having had nothing to do with the stoning. Porteous, who was quickly arrested, tried and found guilty, was sentenced to be hanged on 8 September 1736. With a few behind-the-scenes interventions, he was granted a reprieve of six weeks. The common people of Edinburgh smelt a rat. They thought this was just the first step towards Porteous being eventually pardoned.

On the night of 7 September a large crowd gathered outside the city gates and, led by a drummer, they marched through the West Port and on to the Tolbooth prison where Porteous was being held. Some of them went down the High Street and locked the Netherbow port, thus isolating the troops billeted at the time in the Canongate. They then proceeded to the Tolbooth itself where, by the simple expedient of burning down the doors, they forced an entry. Porteous was dragged from his cell and taken down the West Bow and into the Grassmarket where he had given his fateful order. There he was hung from a dyer's pole close to the official execution site, which can still be seen in today's Grassmarket opposite The Last Drop pub. Then the mob dispersed leaving the body of the unfortunate Porteous twisting in the wind. This had been a remarkable statement of the power of the Edinburgh mob and there was outrage among the ruling class. Despite all their efforts however no one was ever successfully tried for the lynching of John Porteous and the reputation of the Edinburgh mob was greatly enhanced.

It is unclear who the drummer leading the mob was, but another drummer came to prominence leading the Edinburgh mob in later years. This was

Joseph Smith, a belt-maker who got his nickname from the fact that his legs were spectacularly bowed, making him just over four feet tall (1.3m). He lived in Leith Wynd just off the High Street and was very much to the fore in Edinburgh rioting. Various things could set the mob off, including rises in food prices for example, and Joseph was always to the fore. He would come out from his humble dwelling with his drum and proceed to rouse the tenants of the bustling tenements of the Cowgait and the Canongait. He could summon together as many as 10,000 people from the lower classes of the Edinburgh population and on such occasions their so-called betters generally though it best to shut up

▲ The Grassmarket looking west

shop and hide away. For the mob was a fearsome entity once roused, though it is generally believed that Joseph Smith was a man with a strong sense of justice, more concerned with fair play than with the enjoyment of power.

One year, around 1780, a poor man in the Pleasance, having fallen on hard times, could not pay his rent at Martinmas on 1 November so his landlord, showing all the humanity for which those of his profession are so well known, turned the man and his six children out in the street and seized all his worldly goods which were promptly sold to recoup his lost rent. The man, distraught by this catastrophe, killed himself. The word of what had happened soon reached Joseph Smith who immediately went into the streets with his drum. Within 30 minutes or so he had gathered a crowd of thousands and led them to Thomson's Park where he told them what had happened and called for them to follow him in redressing this heinous wrong. So they marched to the landlord's house in the Pleasance and forced their way in. Every stick of furniture and all of his personal possessions were thrown into the street where they were piled up. Joseph then set fire to the heap as a city magistrate and a small group of soldiers looked on, extremely reluctant to become directly involved. Despite there being witnesses at the scene no charges were brought against Joseph or any of his companions.

In fact it seems that Joseph was regularly consulted by the magistrates and councillors of Edinburgh when they thought trouble was looming. A man of considerable intelligence Joseph knew how to turn such occasions to his advantage and on quite a few occasions trouble was averted by his suggesting that a few hogsheads of ale be broached on Calton Hill and the populace invited to have a drink or two. Then Joseph would tell the crowd to go home and trouble would be avoided. After many years as the unofficial leader of the mob Joseph met an untimely death. He fell from the top of a coach coming back from Leith Races after perhaps having had too much to drink and broke his neck. Sadly his skeleton was put on display in the anatomy classes at the university as a curiosity, because of his remarkable bowed legs.

The Edinburgh mob continued to erupt occasionally into the early 19th century but two particularly significant instances relate directly to specific aspects of our trail. The first of these was the King's Birthday Riot of 1792. It was customary for the establishment to celebrate the King's birthday, often paying for the common folk to have a boisterous and inebriated celebration, and in 1792 King George III's birthday fell on 4 June. In the aftermath of the American and French Revolutions there was growing demand for parliamentary reform in Scotland, where literacy had helped Thomas Paine's radical ideas be widely disseminated through the reading of his books *The Age of Reason* and *The Rights of Man*. As such, in the run up to the celebration a number of handbills were printed and circulated round Edinburgh calling for action on the prescribed day. The provost and the town councillors did their best to tear these down whenever they saw them but the ideas of liberty and equality that had been stirred up by Thomas Paine's writings and the French Revolution were not so easily suppressed. It was even advertised in advance that an effigy of Henry Dundas was to be burned at the event. Lord Melville, the despot who ran Scotland as a personal fiefdom was to be publicly burnt. A bill was circulated which called on all those who wished the trade and commerce well to assemble in Antigua Street on Leith Walk on the King's Birthday at 8am. It continued with the somewhat ominous words:

> when we shall give a general Salute in the way it was given to Captain Porteous of the Town Guard, to Mr Maitland, General Supervisor of the Excise.

The reference to Porteous was chilling considering his end, but Maitland was widely accused of taking bribes from the rich and 'skimming the poor'.

The riot started on 4 June and carried on sporadically over the next two days. On the first night there were running skirmishes between the mob and Dragoons, some of whom had been brought from Carlisle to try and control the situation. However the closes and vennels of the High Street made it all too easy for the crowd to scatter and reform and the fun continued until about 2am. On the night of the 5th an effigy of Henry Dundas was burnt in front of his mother's house in George Square. Dundas' nephew Colonel Francis Dundas was injured in the ensuing melee after he and others, including the famous Admiral Duncan – who became a great hero at the subsequent battle of Camperdown against the French – attempted to disperse the crowd. As with the night before, the Riot Act was read and troops called in. The troops managed to clear the area but later that night a group of rioters returned and broke some of the windows of Dundas' mother's house. More rioters began to appear and the troops also returned. The crowd, having faced down the troops several times already, were eventually forced to scatter when they opened fire, killing one man and seriously injuring half a dozen others. The following night the Provost's house in St Andrew's Square was attacked, all its windows were broken but the mob's attempt to set fire to it failed. The Dragoons dispersed the crowd and the three days of rioting were effectively over.

There can be little doubt that the circulation of radical ideas of parliamentary reform played a part on this outbreak of violence and they also probably made the intransigence of Dundas and his minions all the more obdurate. The patronising attitude of the 'leading citizens' was shown at a meeting the following day attended by all the Magistrates. They maintained that:

> certain persons in higher ranks of life not only withheld their assistance… but countenanced the lower ranks by inflaming their minds with seditious opinions.

This was patent nonsense. The idea that the common people could only function when led by their betters flew directly in the face of all evidence about the Edinburgh mob. Despite large financial rewards put on offer, no one came forward to give any information about the rioters and in the end only three people were ever formally charged with taking part in that particular riot. One of them was found guilty of throwing one stone at the soldiers. His name was Alexander Lochie, who had probably been picked out because of the livery he wore as a chaise driver. His lawyer was Thomas Muir of Huntershill, a radical whose activities soon brought him directly up against the entrenched power of Dundas and the corruption of the British State.

In 1796 there was another riot on the King's Birthday. It resulted in some window smashing and general rioting but came nowhere near the intensity of the one in 1792. One can see echoes of the widespread rioting against the Act of Union that had taken place as long ago as 1707 in these outbreaks. However during this time the Edinburgh mob had also come out on many occasions in support of the status quo, but from 1792 this changed. The call for parliamentary reform, although it took another 40 years to be effective, was now part of the political reality of contemporary life. There was clearly a growing level of political awareness, which included direct calls for Scotland to leave the Union from such radicals as James Callender Thomson in his *The Political Progress of Great Britain*, published in America in 1792. Like many others of the time Callender left Scotland for America to avoid the fate that awaited Thomas Muir and others. This book is not available in Scottish libraries, which may be a reflection on the thinking that has always dominated Scottish institutions within the United Kingdom. More recently however, with the restoration of the Scottish Parliament and the 2014 referendum on Scottish independence, radical options have once more come into play and open debate.

CHAPTER SIX

Old Assembly Close

Map Location 6

THE NATIONAL COVENANTS show how important
the Scots legal system continued to be in defining
Scotland, politically and culturally. In this close,
with its 17th century features, we find the Faculty
of Advocates named after Sir George Mackenzie.
He was a leading legal thinker of the 17th century,
a royalist, staunch suppressor of the radically
religious (hence 'Bluidy Mackenzie'), a novelist, and
founder of the precursor of today's National Library
of Scotland.

Standing here shows us that the Scottish
Enlightenment began in the 17th century long before
the 1707 Union. But actually we have to go further
back to understand how Enlightenment and later
political reforms connect with Radical Reformation
ideas, as well as medieval Scottish thinkers. For that
we must consider the story of George Buchanan,
who is every bit as important as John Knox, perhaps
more so in the longer legacy of Scotland's 16th
century upheavals.

Buchanan was a scholar and poet of European
renown, teaching in France and Portugal before
returning to his native Scotland. He was a Christian
Humanist Reformer, which means that his ideas
came from studying the most influential classical and
Biblical texts in their original languages and

reinterpreting their meaning. He also employed drama as an educational tool and in the process founded Europe's neo-classical theatre tradition. In Europe Buchanan was a Catholic Reformer falling foul of the Inquisition, but on coming back to Scotland he became a Protestant and helped the New Kirk reorganise the Scottish Universities.

In Europe Buchanan's poetry was widely lauded and he became a laureate of the young Queen of Scotland and France, Mary Stuart. It was her unforeseen return to Scotland as a widow in 1561 that brought Buchanan back in her train. In Edinburgh he became the leading Court poet and dramatist, but he was also an admirer of Mary's austerely Protestant half-brother, James Stewart Earl of Moray. In addition Buchanan's family had traditional ties of loyalty to the Earl of Lennox, whose son Henry Lord Darnley was to marry the Queen in 1565.

The murder of Darnley and Mary's subsequent deposition provide the controversial background to Buchanan's radical political thought. His *Dialogue on the Law of Kingship among the Scots* was prompted as a defence of the overthrow of a legitimate reigning Queen, and its subsequent influence has been huge. The argument is that rulers and rulers alike are subject to the rule of law, and bound to obey it in the same way. Consequently, while a king is justified in taking strong measures to uphold the law, so his subjects may be justified in defying and even violently dethroning a ruler who is not behaving lawfully. Buchanan anticipates the

◀ Old Assembly Close, High Street

concept of citizen rights, as well as limited or constitutional monarchy. Both come from his dedication to Stoic virtues of reason and discipline, which supposedly flourished in the Roman Republic after kings and before emperors.

Buchanan then goes on to sketch a history of Scottish kingship, based on the sovereignty not of the ruler but of the governed, the people. Legitimacy in Scotland, he argues, has always come from below and not above. As a consummate Humanist Buchanan wrote in Latin; this extract is from a modern translation of *A Dialogue on the Law of Kingship* by Martin S. Smith and Roger A. Mason:

> When our kings are publicly inaugurated, they give a solemn promise to the entire people that they will observe the laws, customs and ancient practices of our ancestors, and that they will adhere to the laws that they have received from them. This is shown by the entire order of ceremonies and by the first visits which the king makes to individual towns. All this makes it easy to see the nature of the power they received from our ancestors, namely, the same as is held by those who, having been chosen by election, swear to observe the laws… These facts make it probable that the power received by our kings from our ancestors was not unbounded but limited and restricted within fixed boundaries. There was, too, the confirmation given by the passage of time and the exercise of this right by the people without interruption, an exercise never censured by any public degree.

This is partly opinion and partly historical theory, on which Buchanan enlarges at length in his *History of Scotland* which he finished in lodgings a little east of here beside the Tron Kirk.

The critical point is that Buchanan's political thought is civic and 'republican', contradicting Knox's notion that resistance to unjust tyrants is justified by the Bible. In fact, Buchanan points out that St Paul explicitly commands obedience to rulers in the New Testament, while arguing that this relates to St Paul's historical situation, and should not be applied to the present day. In this way, Buchanan avoids the dangers of religious fundamentalism, and provides a basis for modern radical thought, as well as some continuity with late medieval Catholic writers such as John Mair. Buchanan's *Law of Kingship* later influenced American constitutional thinking, and has been consistently deployed in favour of Scottish home rule, devolution and independence.

Buchanan was no armchair theorist. He devised the forensic case against Mary Queen of Scots, depicting her not only as a tyrant but as an adulterer and assassin. This was lurid copy, but Buchanan's storyline of an adulterous Queen, who plots to kill her husband the rightful King and supplant him with her lover, is worthy of a neo-classical drama. It also looks like the inspiration for Shakespeare's *Hamlet*, which was written partly to flatter James VI's love of theatre, given his and his Danish Queen's likely succession to the English throne.

The problem is that much of what Buchanan asserts is untrue. Worse, he probably knew that at least some of what he wrote with such devastating effect was both untrue and based on forged or doctored documents. He may even have had a hand in the doctoring. Subsequently Buchanan became senior tutor to James VI, who never forgot the superb grounding in languages, poetry and drama that he gained from the master poet. But equally he never forgave the grumpy old man's beatings, the depiction of his mother as 'a whore', and Buchanan's virulent anti-monarchism.

During his declining years Buchanan focussed on expanding his theory of kingship, and his blackening of Mary's name in his brilliant *History of Scotland*. Despite its clear bias, the book is a great literary work. As it finally went to press Buchanan was very unwell and living in poor circumstances in Kennedy Close, by The Tron. There he was visited by his admirer Andrew Melville and his own nephew Thomas Buchanan. He sent them onto his printer to see how things were progressing, but they returned to say the presses had stopped at Chapter 17, as Arbuthnot the printer was worried about how the now adult King would react to Buchanan's account of the Rizzio murder.

'Have I told the truth?' asked the old controversialist.

'Yes, I think so, sir,' replied his nephew.

'Then I will abide the King's feud and that of all his kin.'

Though a defiant Buchanan died soon afterwards, his *History of Scotland* was quickly suppressed by royal command and copies burned at the Mercat Cross. Soon however it was published in Europe and widely read. As on today's web, ideas have a habit of spreading despite every effort to contain or repress them. Buchanan's influence spread far beyond Scotland.

On the home front Buchanan's ideas were central to the later 1689 Claim of Right, which was passed by a special Convention of the Scottish Estates. This gave legal and constitutional justification for the deposition of James VII (II of England) in favour of the dual monarchy of William and Mary. James had neither abdicated nor been overthrown in Scotland, so it was necessary to show that he had 'forfeited' the crown through unconstitutional behaviour. The Convention consequently claimed the 'right' of the Scottish people to overthrow one monarch and appoint another. James VII was a grandson of Buchanan's reluctant pupil James VI, and the great-grandson of Mary Queen of Scots who had become the focus of his bitter enmity. So the curmudgeonly bones of the old radical may have stirred in his grave at Greyfriars Kirk. It is often forgotten that during her short reign, joint with William of Orange, Mary was in her own right Mary II of Scotland.

CHAPTER SEVEN

New Assembly Close

Map Location 7

FROM OLD TO New Assembly Close is less than 200 yards in distance, but you traverse a century of cultural change. As in James Court an air of space, social order and decorum has intervened, so you can imagine the polite middle classes gathering here to formally dance and politely converse, anticipating the more expansive and ordered New Town of Edinburgh beyond the Nor Loch.

But these changes were politically ambivalent. On one hand the Scottish Enlightenment depended on socio-economic elites to practise and fund its progressive values. Lairds, lawyers and minsters were all to the fore. Consequently there was a need to reform but not to rock established power structures. On the other hand the Enlightenment fostered habits of independent thought and individual freedom, inconsistent with the dominance of professional elites in an 18th century Scotland that was managed at 'a stroke of the pen' from London.

Yet an undercurrent of radical thinking flows on from George Buchanan to the poetry of Robert Burns in the late 18th century, and the progressive social thought of early 19th century philosophers such as Glasgow's John Millar and Edinburgh's

◄ New Assembly Close, High Street

Dugald Stewart. Between them is a key connecting thinker, the Irish Presbyterian Francis Hutcheson, who links the world of the 17th century Covenants and the modern age. Acknowledged by Adam Smith and David Hume as a profound influence, the genial and calmly radical Hutcheson studied in Glasgow, and taught in Dublin for ten years before returning to his alma mater as Professor of Moral Philosophy.

Hutcheson provides a clear, consistent basis for a humane society by arguing that we have an innate moral sense that desires co-operation and harmony. He sees this sense as coming ultimately from God the Creator, but insists that it operates as a human faculty enabling benevolence and social progress, regardless of race or creed.

Such progress does not happen automatically; it requires education, good social and economic organisation, religion that inspires fellow feeling, and the arts. In addition, Hutcheson argues there should be representative political structures with a wide franchise and regular elections, in order that the human potential for cooperation and improvement can be realised, and the restrictive dominance of vested interests avoided.

In the first half of the still hierarchical 18th century, Hutcheson's thought undermines the need for hierarchy and imposed order, which he sees as based on an inadequate understanding of humanity. At the same time he avoids an exclusive or debilitating piety, emphasising instead a shared God-given human potential. In this way Hutcheson pleases neither the privileged nor the pious, but clears an open space of potential for everyone.

Hutcheson's civic humanism owes much to

Buchanan and the classical writers. But unlike Buchanan he emphasises emotion and psychology as positive agents, rather than reason as controlling disordered passions. For Hutcheson reason and reflection are important, but not the deepest or most influential causes of behaviour. Adam Smith and David Hume both build on Hutcheson's thought in this regard, but so did the later 18th century democrats and radicals, including the United Irishmen, the Friends of the People, and the North American constitutionalists. On another front Hutcheson pointed a way forward for Scottish Protestantism beyond the Solemn League and Covenant and the Westminster Confession, which are shaped by the 17th century battlelines. For this service, the good Professor received little thanks from the 'unco godly', then or since.

CHAPTER EIGHT

The Old Calton Hill Burial Ground

Map Location 8

TOWERING ABOVE the tombs and gravestones of Old Calton Cemetery on Regent Road, is an obelisk of grey sandstone that was raised in 1840 by public subscription. It is dedicated to the men known as the Scottish Political Martyrs and is a reminder of the ongoing attachment of Radical and reforming ideas to Calton Hill itself. The Martyrs Thomas Muir, Maurice Margarot, Thomas Fyshe Palmer, Thomas Skirving and Joseph Gerrald were sentenced to transportation for sedition to Botany Bay in Australia in 1793 and 1794. Though they are known as the Scottish Political Martyrs, in fact only Muir and Skirving were Scots. Joseph Gerrald was a West Indian-born English landowner, Maurice Margarot an English Radical of French descent and Thomas Fyshe Palmer was an English Unitarian Clergyman. Muir was a young lawyer originally from Huntershill near Glasgow and William Skirving was a farmer and a tutor from Liberton.

Their crime? Calling for exactly the same kind of reform of the corrupt political system that the then Prime Minister William Pitt had been demanding in

◀ The Political Martyrs' Monument, Old Calton Cemetery

opposition barely more than a decade earlier. In the aftermath of the French Revolution the British Establishment was in a state of panic and when the Societies of Friends of the People held a convention in Edinburgh on 12 December 1792, with delegates from across the country and visiting delegates from fraternal organisations in England and Ireland, a crackdown was inevitable. This crackdown was led by Henry Dundas, Lord Melville, a close associate of William Pitt and a man who had absolute control of all government in Scotland and who hated the Radical reformers with a passion.

The Convention in December 1792 already referred to, led directly to the arrests of Muir and the others and what followed is still a stain on the judicial system in Scotland. Although the people of Scotland have never forgotten the Martyrs, they have been ignored by the establishment and all too many of its lickspittle historians. The extent of this can be shown even today by the fact that the memorial is not even mentioned on the notice board on the gates to Calton Cemetery provided by the Edinburgh City Council. Mention is made of the tomb of the philosopher David Hume and even the monument to the Scots who fought in the American Civil War is referred to, but the monument that soars above all the others has not been deemed worthy of note by the powers that be in Scotland's capital, even yet.

The men were arrested and charged with sedition. During the summer the King's Birthday Riot in Edinburgh had been followed by similar events in

The Political Martyrs' Monument, close-up ▶

Aberdeen, Perth, Dundee and villages throughout the rest of the country, with effigies of Dundas being publicly burned and a considerable amount of public disorder. Alongside these riots there were several instances of Trees of Liberty being erected, perhaps triggered by the victories of the French Revolutionary Government against its enemies. Dundee and Perth were particularly noted for their dissent, with Fyshe Palmer having been to the fore in the Dundee activities. The calls for parliamentary reform were growing stronger and there was only one way Dundas was going to react. The arrest of Muir, Palmer and the others led to a series of trials that were blatantly rigged. The charges were pathetic but by using handpicked juries known for their government sympathies it was ensured that there could only be one outcome. All of the men charged were found guilty. Many of the men on the juries thought that fines or short prison sentences would be a sufficient punishment but they had not allowed for Dundas' brutality.

The sentence handed down was that of transportation for 14 years to Botany Bay, Australia, a sentence that so few ever returned from that it was considered a slow form of the death sentence. Only Muir and Margarot ever saw Europe again. The trials were an international sensation, being followed closely in England, France and extensively in America. In fact Muir's closing speech became a standard part of American teaching, memorised by generations of American schoolchildren while the country of his birth ignored him. This of course was partially the result of the fact that it was only with the introduction of Scottish history as an official part of the 2010 Curriculum for Excellence that any obligation to teach Scottish history to Scottish children began. This is part of that speech:

> As for me I am careless and indifferent to my fate. I can look danger and I can look death in the face, for I am shielded by the consciousness of my own rectitude. I may be condemned to languish in the recesses of a dungeon, I may be doomed to ascend the scaffold; nothing can deprive me of the recollection of the past – nothing can destroy my inward peace of mind arising from the remembrance of having discharged my duty.

The attitude of the Edinburgh populace to the Martyrs can be clearly seen from an incident during the trial of Maurice Margarot in 1794. Margarot's trial was due to start on 13 January. It had been delayed because of him being ill. The supporters of Radicalism had organised a procession to accompany him to the court that Monday. A sizeable crowd turned up that morning at the Black Bull in Leith Street where he was staying. A carriage had been arranged and the gathered crowd removed the horses and a group of young men took their place as a sign of respect to Margarot. The authorities, well aware of what was planned, gathered their own crowd of Magistrates, the Sheriff, the town constables, the trained bands of the city – groups ostensibly organised for the defence of Edinburgh against foreign attack – along with many 'respectable citizens' and over 100 sailors from the naval ships conveniently moored in the Forth.

The procession was met on the North Bridge by the forces of law and order and the banner being carried at the front of the procession was seized. It read, 'Liberty and Virtue, Reason, Justice and

Truth.' Nowadays this may seem almost bland but each and every word sent a chill into Dundas' heart. The procession was violently dispersed and Margarot hauled off to face his own show trial. That night there were sporadic small-scale disturbances but nothing like previous riots occurred. Margarot of course was found guilty and given his 14 years transportation, just like his companions. It is worth recalling that the various trials of Radicals that took place in England at the time led to much less serious punishments, and many staunch supporters of the Government in England were shocked at the barbarity of these sentences.

The blatant repression by the forces of Government had its desired effect and for a considerable period most political reform activity was driven underground, with only sporadic outbursts like the anti-militia riots of 1797. These were triggered by the raising of militias supposedly to defend the country against French invasion, for which service was compulsory. Well it was compulsory for young men whose parents did not possess enough wealth to buy them out of the obligation. One of the riots in 1797, led to Dragoons opening fire on unarmed protesters in Tranent killing a dozen people. No one was ever prosecuted.

Of all of the Scottish Political Martyrs, including others like George Mealmaker of Dundee, who were likewise transported for similar so-called offences in subsequent years, Thomas Muir, the young lawyer from near Huntershill near Glasgow is the best known. This is not just because of his bravery and oratorical skills but because of what subsequently happened to him. He managed to escape from

Botany Bay early in 1796, with rumours flying that American supporters sent a ship out especially to free him. This may have been influenced by the fact that the French Revolutionary Government had made some rather desultory efforts in 1793 to try and intercept the ship that took Muir and his companions out to Australia. Muir had been in France directly before his trial and his support for the principles of the French Revolution was well known.

After a remarkable series of adventures which included discovering a new Pacific island and having a dangerous meeting with indigenous tribespeople near Vancouver, he headed to Mexico, which like most of western America was still under Spanish rule. After initially being treated as an honoured guest he was eventually imprisoned as a dangerous foreign agitator and, after serving some time in prison in Mexico and Cuba, he was sent by the Spanish authorities back to Spain in the ship *Ninfa* carrying a considerable amount of silver and gold. By now Spain had joined France in war with Britain and the *Ninfa* and its companion ship were intercepted off the north-west coast of Spain. In the subsequent battle Muir had half his face blown off and after the Spanish ships were forced to surrender British naval personnel came aboard.

Muir was recognised but he was in such a pitiful state that word was sent back to Scotland that he had in fact died of his wounds. He was sent ashore in a long boat with the Spanish sailors and locked up in a prison in Cadiz. He corresponded with Thomas Paine in France during his slow recovery and when the French Government heard of his situation they sent a diplomatic mission to have him released and brought to Paris. There he was treated like a hero. However his various troubles seem to have affected him rather badly as he was soon badgering the French to send him to Scotland with enough muskets to raise the Scots against the English.

It is sad indictment of too many Scots' awareness of their own history that he remains so little known in his native land. There have long been rumours that Muir met Rabbie Burns and there is little doubt that the poet's great paean to Scottish history, 'Scots Wha Hae', was inspired by the Radicals of the time, though whether the two of them did meet is as yet unproven. The Martyrs, apart from Muir and Margarot all died in the Southern Hemisphere but such was the attachment to their memory that after the passing of the Reform Bill in 1834 (1832 in England) a public declaration of remembrance attracted lots of support throughout Britain. The Radical MP Joseph Hume started a movement to have a monument erected to them in 1837. On 21 August 1844, the foundation stone was laid with over 300 people in attendance. The monument was designed by Thomas Hamilton who also designed the Royal High School and the Burns Monument further east along Regent Road.

CHAPTER NINE

Regent Road, The Governor's House

Map Location 9

THE GOVERNOR'S HOUSE is all that remains of the Old Calton Jail which was demolished in the early 1930s to make way for St Andrew's House, long the seat of bureaucratic Westminster control but now home to the civil servants of the Scottish Parliament. The jail itself was a notably brutal place and in the First World War it held some rather well known prisoners. These included John MacLean, renowned left-wing activist and Willie Gallagher, Scotland's first, and to date, only Communist MP. Along with other supposed ringleaders they were jailed for helping organise a strike in the Glasgow Shipyards. The pay of the shipyard workers had been cut, supposedly because of the war effort, but it was common knowledge that the shipyard owners were receiving vastly inflated profits because of that same war effort. The imprisonment didn't last long once the powers that be realised that the effect on the morale of the shipyard workers of locking up their spokesmen was hardly likely to be conducive to high productivity.

To this day the interests of the rich form the core concern of British Government and it is an absolute commitment of many Scottish nationalists that an independent Scotland will have a more open and equitable government in future. MacLean may indeed have been backing the wrong horse when he accepted the post of the Soviet Union's Ambassador to Scotland in 1918, but he did it out of a commitment to helping improve the lot of the vast majority of the population. And like so many Communists in Scotland, he was committed to using democratic processes, not subverting them, as has too often been the case with our elected politicians. MacLean and Gallagher along with James MacDougall and John Maxton, who also later became an MP, were actually charged with sedition, in a bizarre echo of the persecution of Thomas Muir and the Scottish Political Martyrs. Another of their comrades, Davie Kirkwood, who in time became the Labour peer Lord Kirkwood, was actually deported from Glasgow and imprisoned for some time in Edinburgh Castle. The fight for industrial rights has been as tortuous as that for political reform.

▼ Governor's House

CHAPTER TEN

Calton Hill, The Dugald Stewart Monument

Map Location 10

THE MONUMENT TO Professor Dugald Stewart on the western edge of Calton Hill was modelled on the Choragic Monument to Lysicrates in Athens. The Greek theme so dominant on Calton Hill not only reflects the Western fascination with the ancient Greeks and their civilisation, but also reminds us that Greece itself was long seen as the very fount of democracy itself. The choice of such a specific Greek model is thus quite telling, for in Dugald Stewart we find a man who fought for democratic ideals in his own way. The son of a professor of Mathematics at Edinburgh University, by the time he was in his mid-20s Dugald too was a professor, teaching both mathematics and philosophy.

A great follower of the works of the philosopher Thomas Reid and Adam Smith, Stewart was a man of great erudition and was importantly open-minded and liberal in his approach to learning and teaching. In the fanatical and fearful 1790s when the British Establishment was carrying on its own Reign of Terror against anyone who raised the cry of 'Reform', Dugald was forced to keep his head down.

Even Smith's idea of 'free markets' was deemed revolutionary by the establishment, which seems ironic at a time when the most fervent advocates of the supposed free market constantly use Smith to justify their rapaciousness, all the time ignoring Smith's own dictum 'that men of business should never be allowed into politics.'

By the turn of the new century the worst of the British Government repression was over – though the corruption of Scottish governance was still unaddressed – and Stewart began to broaden the scope of his teachings. In addition to teaching moral philosophy he introduced the new topic of political economy which allowed him to spread Adam

▲ Monument to Dugald Stewart, Calton Hill

Smith's ideas and develop his own thinking. His wide ranging intellect led him to write on many topics apart from mathematics and philosophy and included influential works in the field of linguistics. He was a true polymath. While never ostensibly a Radical he did have some sympathy for the cause of Reform. He was renowned as a speaker and pupils came from as far away as mainland Europe and America to attend his lectures. The influential *Edinburgh Review* was founded in 1802 by a group of his students inspired by his teaching, and soon became an international success, promoting laissez-faire economics and the cause of liberty. Stewart retired in 1801, just as the outbreak of war with France saw further government clampdown on liberal and reforming ideas.

This in turn led to a counter-revolution against the Moderatism of the Presbyterian Church and a subsequent purging of the ideas of Adam Smith and Robert Fergusson et al, which Dugald Stewart had done so much to propagate. The sceptical, moderate and progressive agenda of Stewart was swept aside and strict theological control of the faculties of philosophy in Scotland's universities was reintroduced. The immediate result was that these institutions lost their philosophical vigour and fell back from their position as world centres of intellectual excellence. It wasn't until 1831, just a year before the Reform Act of 1832 was passed in Westminster that the monument to Stewart was raised, three years after his death. Eventually his legacy was to prevail inspiring Scotland's later 19th century intellectual development.

There is no commemoration on Calton Hill to

another event of some significance that took place here. On 15 September 1834 a great pavilion was erected on the hill, close to the Royal High School for a celebratory dinner. The guest of honour was Earl Grey who two years earlier had pushed through the Reform Bill, which had at long last addressed the corruption at the heart of British governance. The buying and selling of parliamentary seats was outlawed, the franchise greatly extended and the groundwork laid for the journey towards the universal franchise. At the time over 15,000 people had marched through Edinburgh and it was after this famous banquet that the MP Joseph Hume started the agitation for the Martyr's Monument.

CHAPTER ELEVEN

Calton Hill, The Vigil Cairn

Map Location 11

THE VIGIL CAIRN was raised by the supporters of The Vigil for a Scottish Parliament which began after the unexpected Conservative victory in the 1992 UK General election. There is a fuller eyewitness account of the Vigil in the next section. In particular the cairn commemorates the Democracy Marches of April 1993 which saw groups come from the furthest points of Scotland north, south, east and west, to meet here on the first anniversary of the founding of the Vigil. Some of these journeys took several weeks and involved local events raising both funds and consciousness along the way. Many people also walked alongside the marchers for short distances to show their support for the struggle for a Scottish Parliament.

Vigil supporters held many events on the top of Calton Hill, complementing their permanent presence on Regent Road opposite the gates of the Old Royal High School. The political name taken by the Vigil supporters, Democracy for Scotland, was a clear statement of just what was being fought for and reflected the growing frustration that Scotland was being governed by a Conservative party whose policies had been repeatedly and overwhelmingly rejected by the electorate.

For we hae faith
In Scotland's hidden poo'ers,
The present's theirs
but a' the past and future's oors.

Hugh MacDiarmid

The idea of a democratic deficit in Scotland had long taproots in previous Home Rule movements. In the modern period, after the Second World War, two million adults signed the Scottish Covenant calling for self-government. The final text was agreed by a National Assembly of the Scottish Convention held in the General Assembly Hall. This expression of popular will was ignored by the postwar Labour Government. In the 1950s the movement subsided, despite the symbolic impact of the removal of the Stone of Destiny from Westminster Abbey in 1950.

Renewed agitation came with the rise of Scottish Nationalism in the 1970s, with a string of election successes alarming the established political order. In 1979 the devolved Scottish Assembly proposed by the Labour Party in response to Nationalism was derailed at Westminster by backbench resistance. In the same year the Conservatives led by Margaret Thatcher came to power. A cross-party and civic campaign for a Scottish Assembly began, leading in 1988 to the publication of *A Claim of Right for Scotland*. This restates the principle of the sovereignty of the people on whose assent all structures of government should rest, so consciously echoing the 1689 Claim of Right Act:

> We, gathered as the Scottish Constitutional Convention, do hereby acknowledge the sovereign right of the Scottish people to determine the form of government best suited to their needs, and do hereby declare and pledge that in all our actions and deliberations their interests shall be paramount.

◄ The Vigil Cairn, Calton Hill

We further declare and pledge that our actions and
deliberations shall be directed to the following ends:

To agree a scheme for an Assembly or Parliament for
Scotland

To mobilise Scottish opinion and ensure the approval of the
Scottish people for the scheme; and

To assert the right of the Scottish people to secure
implementation of that scheme.

The Scottish Constitutional Convention was formed
to advance the principles set out in the Claim of
Right Act. This began with all the political parties
involved, with the exception of the Conservatives,
but the Scottish National Party left when the
Convention refused to include independence as one
route by which the democratic deficit could be
addressed.

The Convention published its blueprint for a
devolved Scottish parliament in 1995, *Scotland's
Parliament, Scotland's Right*, which was influential
on the form of devolution subsequently enacted in
1997. However by 1995 the Vigil's Democracy for
Scotland movement had revealed a grassroots
appetite for democratic change, and was successfully
keeping the cause before the public eye.

CHAPTER TWELVE

Regent Road, The Vigil Plaque

Map Location 12a

OPPOSITE ST ANDREW'S HOUSE and just to the left of the road leading up to the hilltop from the entrance gate to the old Royal High School, there is a small brass plaque on the wall. This commemorates a unique event in Scotland's political history that both drew on and continued the Radical theme. On 10 April 1992 Scotland had voted out the Conservatives and England had voted them in. Thus Scotland, one of the constituent nations of the United Kingdom of Great Britain and Northern Ireland, had no democratic involvement in the governance of the United Kingdom.

A demonstration against this blatant lack of democracy had been organised by SCRAM, the Scottish Campaign to Remove the Atomic Menace, an anti-nuclear group based in Caithness. They came down to hold a weekend of protest outside the gates of the Royal High School. To gather support they used the phone trees of the CND and anti-Poll tax movement and on the night around 300 people turned up to voice their dissatisfaction with the British system of government which once again had shown its incapacity to deal with the realities of Scottish political life. Despite the frustrations it was a joyous event and in the course of that night discussions arose as to the possibility of making the demonstration a permanent Vigil. Some people were inspired by the ship workers of Gdansk in Poland and their organisation called Solidarity, while others were simply intent on doing something. There was feeling that too many demonstrations, no matter how big, were deemed irrelevant by a political system totally out of touch with the people it claimed to be representing.

The result of this was a permanent protest that lasted five years; a constant reminder of the people's demand for real democracy. At first some of the political parties tried to guide what was happening but it became obvious within a short time that this was not going to be a standard political protest. An organisation was formed called Democracy for Scotland, with people in elected positions, but it was soon realised by the people volunteering to do two hour, or overnight shifts at the Vigil, that things had to be much more loosely organised. It developed into an exercise in people power with all decisions regarding activities made by a vote round the Vigil fire. This was an oil drum with wood burning in it, kept alight to symbolise the flame of democracy.

In itself the Vigil fire became a potent symbol of aspirational politics and the involvement of people individually. Joiners and shopfitters, gardeners and lorry drivers regularly dropped off wood to keep the fire going, all involved through word of mouth. Within a couple of weeks of people sleeping on the street, the singer Pat Kane of Hue and Cry made a donation that enabled a second-hand Portakabin to be brought on site, which made things a lot more comfortable for those hardy souls prepared to do overnight shifts. One of the present writers, Stuart McHardy, was an active volunteer. It should be said that from the beginning the then Lothian Regional Council Labour administration was helpful to the protesters. Even the police, not normally known to like street demonstrations, were remarkably sympathetic.

On 12 December 1992 the Democracy March calling for a Scottish Parliament assembled on Regent's Road and the Vigil itself was hive of activity with a rock band playing and lots of people contributing money. There was also a great trade in Vigil merchandise featuring cups, badges and t-shirts. Organisations involved in the March included the Scottish Trades Union Congress (STUC), Scottish Churches, the Campaign for a Scottish Parliament, Scotland United, the National Union of

▼ Yes Rally, Regent Road, September 2013

Students, Common Cause and the Vigil's Democracy for Scotland campaign.

The march was chaired by the STUC and attended by cross-party politicians and activists including Acting Shadow Scottish Secretary Henry McLeish, Scottish Liberal Democrat leader Jim Wallace, the Scottish National Party's Alex Salmond, Isobel Lindsay from the Campaign for a Scottish Assembly, and writer William McIlvanney. The march ended on the Meadows with a series of speeches and the Vigil was represented on the platform by Hamish Henderson who was a stalwart supporter, and fronted many events for the Vigil. At several other demonstrations at the time, Vigil representatives were not allowed to speak, presumably because the political parties involved were frightened by an organisation that did not conform to their ideas of how democracy should function. While this was resented it did not deflect the Vigil volunteers from doing what they did, keeping up the presence on Regent Road as a constant reminder of Scotland's democratic deficit.

The extent of that democratic deficit showed in other ways. Aware of the remarkable anniversary of the Democracy March, 200 years to the day after Thomas Muir had addressed the Convention in James Court, a briefing paper was put together for the media. Now the media love an anniversary, but it appears not this one. Every media outlet in the capital of Scotland, print and broadcast, including the BBC funded by public subscription, had this briefing paper hand-delivered in the days leading up to the march. The result? Nothing appeared anywhere. There is no need to censor those who know how to censor themselves. The reaction of the Establishment against the Radicals in the 1790s found a sinister echo in the closing years of the 20th century in supposedly modern, democratic Britain.

Scotland United had become the biggest organisation in a series of large demonstrations in various parts of the country, until, after 18 months with no warning whatsoever two co-ordinators who worked for a then Labour MP both quit on the same day. Scotland United collapsed overnight and one can only assume that this had been foreseen. The MP concerned was George Galloway, arch-enemy of the Establishment. However the death of devolution was not assured.

Over the next five years the excitement continued and people came from all over Scotland to do shifts, some on a regular basis. Occasionally visitors from abroad would show up to give support and a few even did shifts themselves, which was always welcome as at times there was a possibility that the fire could be left unattended. The idea that there was no hierarchy and no party political agenda ensured that people from all political viewpoints and walks of life felt they could make a contribution. It was always political but never party political, even though several local councillors were initially heavily involved. The only party leader who showed his face and completed a shift was Alex Salmond. Despite his high profile status he was treated the same as everybody else.

It was often a lonely experience sitting by the fire on Regent Road as on many occasions there was only one person available to do the shift. There were those who lived close by who turned up time and again, but there were always those making great efforts to come from afar. The artist and sculptor George Wyllie made a notable contribution setting up a wooden cannon pointed straight at St Andrew's House (Map Location 12b), which was still the bureaucratic centre of Westminster control of Scotland at this time. He also designed some of the Vigil merchandise. It was always the intention of the Vigil volunteers to avoid being seen to be stuffy or pompous, something that politicians seem unable to avoid, and this led to various fancy dress affairs, history lectures and impromptu music sessions whenever a crowd gathered. One of these events was the Not the Royal Garden Party held in 1996 to coincide with the Establishment parade that flocks to Holyrood when the Queen throws her annual garden party. On one notable occasion a couple of people actually came from the Holyrood bash to put some money in the Vigil tin. In true Vigil style they were accused – in a light-hearted fashion – of doing it to salve their consciences.

What was remarkable about the Vigil was how it was perceived by Scots from all shades of the political spectrum. Stuart McHardy was sitting there on his own one day in 1993 when a Mercedes drew to a halt in the road. Out stepped a lady of some years, dressed in twin-set and pearls and with perfectly coiffed hair of a blueish tinge. She came up to him and said, 'I am a lifelong Conservative but I have to say that what you people are doing is absolutely admirable and I agree with your aims.' She then put a £20 note into the collecting tin which was always to hand, and left, smiling.

At the time the media were going through a

process of what can only be described as 'extreme dumbing down' and the Vigil came to play a key role. From the start there had been the street events like Not the Royal Garden Party, democracy marches and concerts on the top of Calton Hill, but suddenly their role was different. With the dumbing down of the press in particular it became almost a hard and fast rule in the newspapers that every story had to have an accompanying image. So whenever there was any mention of devolution, a photographer would be sent to the Vigil to get the necessary picture. As a result the Vigil became representative of the national struggle for devolution. Of course, this is not the only reason devolution refused to die but it is a key part of the story. The Vigil lasted until the 1997 election results were announced, by which time the late leader of the Labour Party, John Smith, had committed to the establishment of a Scottish Parliament. However, most of the people who attended the Vigil believed that the party's upper echelons had tried to destroy the devolution movement some four years earlier.

To keep boredom at bay, people at the Vigil would discuss all aspects of Scottish culture and there were impromptu casual classes where Thomas Muir and John Maclean were the topics. The Vigil laid a wreath of white roses at the Martyrs' Monument every 12 December.

Always conscious of the Vigil's origins, supporters regularly toured Scotland at weekends with the Vigil tent. This was set up in prominent places in cities and towns to gather signatures for the petition for a Scottish Parliament and, of course, to gather funds. It was used from September 1993 to

The Vigil for a Scottish Parliament began within hours of the election of the UK's fourth consecutive Conservative Government. These governments were opposed to any form of home rule for Scotland. Three quarters of the votes just cast in Scotland had gone to parties supporting the re-establishment of a Scottish Parliament.

The Vigil was kept here daily from the 10th of April 1992 until the results of the Devolution Referendum of 11th September 1997 were declared. People from all over Scotland had voted three to one in favour of restoring their own parliament.

Erected by Democracy for Scotland, 10th April 1998

September 1997 when the Vigil eventually finished, and after 1980 days its work was done. The tent later became part of a democracy exhibit in the new Museum of Scotland.

The Vigil was democracy in action, and just as it had arisen from nowhere so it disappeared once its work was finished. Throughout those five years all those who contributed, no matter how much or how little, were part of something that was essentially of the people, and no one tried to make political capital out of it. Party politicians and the media did not like the idea of the Vigil, but it is to be hoped that in time to come all those who helped it struggle through those five long years will get some sort of recognition beyond the plaque on Regent Road and the cairn on Calton Hill.

▲ The Vigil Plaque, Regent Road

SCOTLAND'S DEMOCRACY TRAIL

CHAPTER THIRTEEN

Regent Road, The Royal High School

Map Location 13

LIKE MANY OF the monuments on Calton Hill the Royal High School is modelled on ancient Greek architecture. Its architect, Thomas Hamilton, based his design on the Temple of Hephaestus in Athens, and it has been justly described as the finest building of the Greek revival in Scotland. During the Enlightenment period in Edinburgh there had been considerable discussion among philosophers of ideas of Greek democracy. This was intellectual posturing, as the majority of them were happy enough to accept the squalid and venal government of the time. The Royal High School was built between 1826 and 1829, during which time the movement towards parliamentary reform was becoming irresistible.

The building was left empty in 1968 when its pupils moved to a new building in Barnton. During the agitation for a devolved Scottish Assembly in the 1970s the building was proposed as the location and was duly refurbished in expectation of a Yes vote. However democracy has never been straightforward in the Westminster system. In the 1978 vote in the House of Commons on the Scotland Act, George Cunningham, a Scottish born Labour Party MP representing the Islington and South Finsbury

constituency in London, added an amendment to the enabling bill.

Backbench Labour MPs united with the Conservatives and the amendment was accepted and duly passed. It stated for the first and only time to date that a British electoral vote should not be judged on a first-past-the-post basis. If the votes for a Scottish Assembly as it was then known, fell short of 40 per cent of the total electorate, the vote would be null and void. The Yes votes cast outnumbered the No with a clear majority, but this manifestation of the democratic will of the Scottish people was not enough to overcome the anti-democratic influence of what is after all constantly trumpeted as the 'Mother of Parliaments.'

The Labour Government was already in crisis, depending on a pact with the Liberals to stay in

▲ The Royal High School, Calton Hill
Courtesy of Kim Traynor, Wikimedia Commons

power, and they lost a vote of confidence in the Commons after the SNP withdrew its support. The ensuing general election ushered in the Thatcher administration. George Cunningham himself subsequently jumped ship to join the short-lived Social Democrat Party which led to him losing his position as an MP.

Eventually, after the decades of struggle to establish a Scottish Parliament, the 1997 Labour Party victory at the 1997 UK general election paved the way for a new Scotland Act and a second devolution referendum. This was overwhelmingly carried at the ballot box in the same year, after a cross party Yes campaign backed by the Scottish National Party, Labour and the now Liberal Democrats.

In these developments Tony Blair, ably backed by his Scottish Secretary Donald Dewar, were resolutely loyal to the commitment of the previous Labour leader John Smith, whose early death had frustrated his unwavering desire to see devolution delivered. Nonetheless, the parliament that devolution established in Edinburgh in 1999 did not realise all the aims of the Claim of Right or the Scottish Constitutional Convention. Canon Kenyon Wright, who was Convener of the Convention throughout its working life detailed these differences, in an analysis of 'unfinished business' during the 2014 independence referendum.

Firstly Wright argues that the 1997 Scotland Act remains rooted in the English idea of the sovereignty of the Crown which is vested in the Westminster Parliament. This includes the unelected House of Lords, and 'My Government' as the Queen refers to her duly elected administration at the opening of Parliament. That version of top down power explains why, for example, a British Prime Minister can declare war without a parliamentary vote, though recent practice in the 'unwritten constitution' has edged towards the need for such a vote. These factors indicate that devolution from Westminster is just that – the granting or conceding of the sovereign power of the UK and not a recognition of the sovereignty of the people of Scotland.

This leads on to Kenyon Wright's second point, which is that if such powers are conceded on Westminster's terms they can also be withdrawn in the same way. In this regard the 1997 devolution settlement fails one of the Scottish Constitutional Convention's key requirements, namely that the powers of the Scottish Parliament cannot be altered without the consent of that parliament. The absence of a written United Kingdom constitution secures the ability of any Westminster Parliament to reverse the decisions of its predecessors if a majority of votes are cast on the day.

In practical terms moreover the overall budget of Holyrood is still in 2014 decided by Westminster, through an annual allocation decided by the London Government and approved on a UK basis. Without tax raising powers the Scottish Parliament is perpetually subsidiary to resource decisions made elsewhere. American colonists argued for 'no taxation without representation', but Scotland's parliament provides representation without taxation, or the associated disciplines. This point is central to any further 'Scotland Acts' conceding more powers to the Scottish Parliament.

Thirdly, in Wright's view, the aim of the Scottish Constitutional Convention to foster a less confrontational and more locally representative democratic process remains unfinished business. Until Scotland can achieve a distinctive constitution based on 'bottom up' sovereignty, real and lasting change cannot be embedded in a different kind of political culture.

Kenyon Wright's conclusion therefore is that the aims and principles of the Convention can only be fulfilled by independence. One could argue that a federal UK with a written constitution could also provide solutions to these issues. Yet genuine federalism would require much greater and more radical change across the United Kingdom, and particularly in England, than Scottish independence. Given the virulent opposition in Britain to European federalism, internal federal constitutional reform seems a forlorn hope short of revolution. Advocates of greater devolution also have to acknowledge that their preferences would be constrained and restricted by a sovereign Westminster.

Despite these overall strictures it is important to recognise that the devolution of powers in 1997 was much greater than what had been envisaged in 1978. In addition the already separate legal system in Scotland enhances the ability of the legislature to influence Scottish society. From the start the Scottish Parliament was more influential than the sum of its significant powers. When the Scottish Executive designated in the 1997 Scotland Act became the Scottish Government on the initiative of First Minister Henry McLeish, popular consent supported and to a degree created the change.

In one other dramatic regard the 1999 Parliament outgrew the devolvers. Some favoured the Royal High School as the correct democratic location for the new Parliament, recognising the long struggle to reach this goal. It has been suggested that Calton Hill was not chosen because of its nationalist symbolism rather than its practical drawbacks. If so, deciding to build a new Parliament at Holyrood was to turn into a much greater national statement. In the meantime, however, in an apt historic touch, the new Parliament began business in the Kirk's General Assembly Hall, where the Scottish Constitutional Convention had also formed its key declarations. The move in due course to the Holyrood building would mark a decisive shift away from Scotland's cultural Calvinism, reflecting perhaps a unique mix in the founding First Minister, Donald Dewar, of Presbyterian principle and unexpressed imaginative passion.

CHAPTER FOURTEEN

Regent Road, The Burns Monument

Map Location 14

It is an ironic aside on Edinburgh society's priorities that the monument to Scotland's, and some might suggest the world's favourite poet, Robert Burns, is hidden away along Regent Road while the one to Sir Walter Scott towers over the main thoroughfare of Princes Street. Scott of course, despite his lifelong interest in Scottish history, was an Edinburgh lawyer par excellence and a fully paid-up member of the Establishment of his time. His importance in the development of the historical novel is undoubtedly significant, Mark Twain even going so far as to blame him for the American Civil War in his *Life on the Mississippi*:

> Sir Walter had so large a hand in making Southern character, as it existed before the war, that he is in great measure responsible for the war. It seems a little harsh toward a dead man to say that we never should have had any war but for Sir Walter; and yet something of a plausible argument might, perhaps, be made in support of that wild proposition. The Southerner of the American Revolution owned slaves; so did the Southerner of the Civil War: but the former resembles the latter as an Englishman resembles a Frenchman. The change of character can be traced rather more easily to Sir Walter's influence than to that of any other thing or person.

Burns on the other hand was anything but an Establishment figure. His poetic genius upset the literati of Edinburgh, succumbing as they were in the late 18th century to English notions of class, as they found it offensive that a man who, as a tenant farmer, actually worked with his hands, yet was a far better poet than any of them. He was also man of distinct Radical tendencies. His genius lay in his ability to understand what is referred to as 'the common man', and in this regard he had been exposed to the ideas of liberty and equality that ran through the works of Thomas Paine, *The Age of Reason* and *The Rights of Man*. Paine was an active propagator of both the American and French Revolutions and highly influential in both. His works sold by the thousands in Scotland in the 1790s and in that great anthem to humanity 'A Man's a Man For Aa That', Burns put Paine's ideas in concise and, to this day, heart-stirring language that makes this song an anthem for all mankind (and a pretty fair candidate for the National Anthem of an independent Scotland).

Burns' popularity in his own lifetime and immediately after his death was remarkable, as the spread of Burns Clubs and Societies across the globe in the early year of the 19th century attest. Now some have said that he was anything but a Radical. He accepted a job as an exciseman working for the Government and people have quoted the poem 'Does Haughty Gaul Invasion Threat?' as evidence of his loyalty to the British state and proof that he was anti-French, anti-Radical and pro-British. Well the last lines of that particular poem tell us much:

But while we sing 'God save the King,'
We'll ne'er forget The People!

This puts him right alongside Thomas Muir and the other Radicals of the 1790s. They were calling for reform not, despite the false charges of sedition brought against them, for revolution, and always stressed the need to use parliamentary methods to reform Parliament itself. The rabid fanaticism of the Establishment flunkeys like Lord Braxfield, who sent the Martyrs to Botany Bay believing his and his friends' privileges to be under threat, preferred to ignore this reality.

When writing to his publisher, Thomson, in September 1793 Burns used these words:

▲ The Burns Monument

▲ Statue of Thomas Paine, Thetford
Courtesy of Andrewself, Wikimedia Commons

SCOTLAND'S DEMOCRACY TRAIL

This thought, in my solitary wanderings, warmed me to a pitch of enthusiasm on the theme of Liberty and Independence, which I threw into a kind of Scottish ode, fitted to the air, that one might suppose to be the gallant Royal Scot's address to his heroic followers on that eventful morning.

BRUCE TO HIS TROOPS

On the Eve of the Battle of Bannockburn
Hey tuttie tattie.
Scots, wha hae wi' Wallace bled, (etc.)
So may God ever defend the cause of Truth and Liberty, as He did that day! – Amen.
PS – I showed the air to Urbani, who was highly pleased with it, and begged me to make soft verses for it; but I had no idea of giving myself any trouble on the subject, till the accidental recollection of that glorious struggle for freedom, associated with the glowing ideas of some other struggles of the same nature, not quite so ancient, roused my rhyming mania. Clarke's set of the tune, with his bass, you will find in the Museum; though I am afraid that the air is not what will entitle it to a place in your elegant selection.

The sentiments of 'Scots Wha Hae', and 'Such a Parcel of Rogues in a Nation', in which he excoriates those who signed the Treaty of Union, show where his true political feelings lay. This is particularly clear in 'The Tree of Liberty', which generations of scholars denied as being written by him despite its clear alignment with Burns' known views. He was very much a Radical and songs like 'Scots Wha Hae', written with Muir et al in mind, and 'A Man's A Man For Aa That', directly inspired as they were by the writings of Thomas Paine, continue to inspire people all over the world today.

THE TREE OF LIBERTY

Heard ye o the tree o France,
I watna what's the name o't;
Around the tree the patriots dance,
Weel Europe kens the fame o't.

It stands where ance the Bastille stood,
A prison built by kings, man,
When Superstition's hellish brood
Kept France in leading-strings, man.

Upo' this tree there grows sic fruit,
Its virtues aw can tell, man;
It raises man aboon the brute,
It maks him ken himsel, man.

Gif ance the peasant taste a bit,
He's greater than a Lord, man,
And wi the beggar shares a mite
O aw he can afford, man.
This fruit is worth aw Afric's wealth,

To comfort us 'twas sent, man:
To gie the sweetest blush o health,
And mak us aw content, man.

It clears the een, it cheers the heart,
Maks high and low gude friends, man;
And he wha acts the traitor's part,
It to perdition sends, man.

My blessings aye attend the chiel,
Wha pities Gallia's slaves, man,
And staw a branch, spite o the deil,
Frae yont tho western waves, man.

Fair Virtue water'd it wi care,
And now she sees wi pride, man,
How weel it buds and blossoms there,
Its branches spreading wide, man.

But vicious folk aye hate to see
The works o Virtue thrive, man;
The courtly vermin's banned the tree,
And grat to see it thrive, man.

King Loui' thought to cut it down,
When it was unco sma', Man,
For this the watchman cracked his crown,
Cut off his head and aw man.

A wicked crew syne, on a time,
Did tak a solemn aith, man,
It ne'er should flourish to its prime,
I wat they pledged their faith, man.

Awa they gaed wi mock parade,
Like beagles hunting game, man,
But soon grew weary o the trade,
And wished they'd been at hame, man.

Fair freedom, standing by the tree,
Her sons did loudly caw, man;
She sang a song o liberty,
Which pleased them ane and aw man.

By her inspired the new-born race
Soon grew the avenging steel, man;
The hirelings ran – her foes gied chase,
And banged the despot weel, man.

Let Britain boast her hardy oak,
Her poplar and her pine, man,
Auld Britain ance could crack her joke,
And o'er her neighbours shine, man.

But seek the forest round and round,
And soon 'twill be agreed, man,
That sic a tree can not be found,
'Twixt London and the Tweed, man.

Without this tree, alake this life
Is but a vale o woe, man;
A scene o sorrow mixed wi strife,
Nae real joys we know, man.

We labour soon, we labour late,
To feed the titled knave, man;
And aw the comfort we're to get
Is that ayont the grave, man.

Wi plenty o sic trees, I trow,
The warld would live in peace, man;
The sword would help to mak a plough,
The din o war wad cease man.

Like brethren wi a common cause,
We'd on each other smile, man;
And equal rights and equal laws
Wad gladden every isle, man.

Wae worth the loon wha wadna eat
Sic halesome dainty cheer, man;
I'd gie my shoon frae aff my feet,
To taste sic fruit, I swear, man.

Syne let us pray, auld England may
Sure plant this far-famed tree, man;
And blythe we'll sing, and hail the day
That gave us liberty, man.

CHAPTER FIFTEEN

Regent Road Park, The Stones of Scotland

Map Location 15

HEADING EAST FROM the Burns monument, in the small park on the same side of the road is an intriguing setting of stones. Known as the Stones of Scotland this monument was created by the sculptors and artists George Wyllie and Kenny Munro in 2002. It was created to celebrate the opening of the Scottish Parliament on 9 October 2004. Around the circle of white stone chippings with a Scots pine in the middle are set 32 stones. Each one comes from the local authority that it represents. In the centre of the circle is another stone slab with the shape of a footprint carved in it. This is a direct reference to places like Dunadd in Argyll and Dunino Den in Fife where such footprints were probably used in the inaugurations of powerful leaders. So with all the stones Wyllie was creating a physical representation of Scotland and with the footprint he was referring back to our long history, a history in which the inauguration of leaders was rooted in a tribal society, which always contained an element of election in their choosing.

Wyllie wanted people to come and place their foot here and saw the installation itself, overlooking the Scottish Parliament as it does, as a 'stone

soapbox' where anyone could say whatever they wanted. He described it as:

> a mini-parliament. People can come along and put their foot in the stone and make a wee speech – the ordinary guy saying what he thinks about the parliament.

This stone also has an inscription from the poet Tessa Ransford, that reads 'whose the tread that fits this mark?'.

Fervently democratic and anti-elitist in his views, Wyllie was in part inspired by a line from Hugh MacDiarmid's poem *Scotland* in which he referred to a 'a statue carved out in a whole country's marble'. Another slab has these lines from MacDiarmid's poem:

▲ The Stones of Scotland, Regent Road

So I have gathered unto myself
All the loose ends of Scotland
And by naming them and accepting them,
Loving them and identifying myself with them,
Attempt to express the whole.

With its view over the Scottish Parliament, a modern, almost futuristic building, and the looming majesty of Arthur's Seat, the Stones of Scotland represent the existence of the nation within a locale that both harks back to our cultural and historic past and forwards to a future Scotland in which democratic ideals and aspirations of equality and fairness will be at the heart of governance.

▲ The old quarry face at Tormore – a block of this stone can be seen in The Stones of Scotland sculpture in Regent Road Park
Courtesy of Malcolm Morris, Geograph

CHAPTER SIXTEEN

Holyrood

Map Location 16

In the medieval period Parliament was convened occasionally as a consultative forum for Royal Government, often at Holyrood Palace. Later it evolved in Scotland into a larger gathering of the Three Estates of the Realm. As previously mentioned the State Opening of Parliament in London still openly demonstrates a royal origin and prerogative. In Edinburgh the much more muted ceremonial opening also acknowledges the place of the

◀ The debating chamber of the Scottish Parliament, Holyrood
Courtesy of Colin, Wikimedia Commons

▲ The Scottish Parliament from Regent Road

monarchy. The Queen is present but is very careful not to claim any ownership of government or parliament. The Scottish crown is brought from Edinburgh Castle in a distant echo of the medieval idea that without the presence of the Monarch, symbolically or physically, parliament could not legitimately meet.

Locating the new Scottish Parliament at Holyrood aligned it with a national tradition firmly rooted in Scotland's existence as a fully independent country. When the site was then combined with the flamboyant talent and ambition of Catalan architect Enrico Miralles, the scene was set for something exceptional and so it transpired.

The commissioning body was the Parliament itself, which of course had no experience of such a

▼   The Scottish Parliament

process or of managing contracts. A mess ensued in which creative ambition, contract management and the budget were all out of sync with each other. The resultant farrago brought devolution into an early crisis of repute, and the difficulties were compounded when Miralles tragically fell ill and died. Great credit goes to the Parliament's Presiding Officer George Reid, who took the crisis into his own hands and eventually brought the tortured process to a conclusion with a resonant opening in 2004.

People remain divided about the design and resentful of the initial cost of the Holyrood Parliament. Yet the Debating Chamber is an undoubted triumph, while the bold synergy between the building and its natural setting of sea, sky and mountain says something essential about Scotland's

▼ The Scottish Parliament, detail, High Street

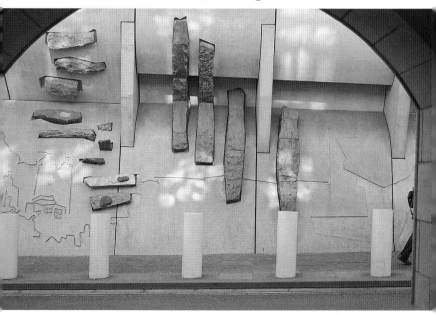

identity. As thousands of visitors mill around the traditional palace and the contemporary parliament, they are vividly connected with the history and the ongoing making of a nation.

If the Miralles building at Holyrood represents a leap of the imagination, then the political development of the new legislature was also unpredicted. Elected through a mixed first past the post and proportional representation system, the aim was to avoid dominance by any one political party. This turned out as intended in the first Scottish Election with a Labour-Liberal Democrat coalition majority, an SNP opposition, and a healthy cluster of minority parties including the Greens and the Scottish Socialist Party. From the outset this was a different dynamic from Westminster.

But things happened. Donald Dewar had a heart attack and then died suddenly soon after returning to work. His able successor Henry McLeish mishandled a minor problem about constituency expenses and resigned. The coalition was then led by First Minister Jack McConnell who led a competent reforming administration that lacked political character or sparkle. This also reflected a problem in the Labour Party who continued with a London-led structure that was not prepared to concede any independent direction to Scotland.

In 2005 the Scottish National Party defeated Labour to become the largest party at Holyrood. The Liberal Democrats also performed poorly and, refusing an SNP coalition partnership, retired to their tents. That decision may yet prove the long-term undoing of the Scottish Liberals, as the SNP formed a minority government and performed with great skill and coherence throughout their four-year term. Against all expectations, the SNP won an outright majority in 2009, campaigning on a raft of distinctive Scottish policies including the pledge to hold an independence referendum.

Of course the 2009 Scottish election was not a vote for independence. The SNP's success is down to their performance in government and their political skill in positioning themselves as the party for Scotland, unlike their 'London established' opponents. But history is not fashioned solely by political astuteness. The Scottish electorate had decided that Holyrood was its government and that it should play a bigger part. This underlying sense of direction was reaffirmed with the return of the Conservative Party to power at Westminster in coalition, unfortunately for their Scottish colleagues, with the Liberal Democrats.

The banking led recession, reductions in the public sector, austerity, growing inequality, and the rise of anti-European feeling over these years seems to have widened rather than narrowed the political and social gap between Westminster and Holyrood. What that means for the evolution of Scottish democracy remains to be seen, but the independence referendum on 18 September 2014 marked a historic milestone on Scotland's Democracy Trail. It has been the most critical juncture since the 1707 Scots Parliament voted itself out of existence.

The history of the 2014 referendum on Scottish independence remains to be written. The result was 55 per cent No to independence and 45 per cent Yes. Over 93 per cent of those eligible to vote were registered, including for the first time 16 and 17 year olds. Argument will continue to rage about the last gasp intervention of the three main Westminster political parties – Conservative, Labour and Liberal Democrat – 'vowing' to deliver greatly increased powers for the Scottish Parliament in the event of a No vote. The role of former UK Prime Minister Gordon Brown as spokesperson for this offer had eerie echoes of the last minute intervention in the 1979 devolution referendum by former UK Prime Minister Sir Alex Douglas-Home, likewise offering a better devolution deal in return for a No vote. Controversy will also continue regarding the perceived bias of the mainstream media, including the BBC, and the open collusion between large UK companies and the Westminster Government in predicting economic woes in the event of a Yes vote.

Nonetheless the 1.6 million Yes voters outnumber by three to one any previous parliamentary vote in favour of parties advocating independence for Scotland. In the wake of the defeat Yes campaigners have flocked to join the Scottish National Party, the Scottish Greens and the Scottish Socialist Party. Moreover with the younger generations strongly weighted on the Yes side while the over 50s stuck with caution, the stage is set for the politics of change in Scotland. If the intention of the referendum was to close down radical debate about Scotland's future, then it has been a signal failure, more of a starting gun than a finish line defeat.

The 2014 campaign outgrew conventional party politics and the mainstream media to involve a whole society in open discussion, questioning and reflection. People were fully aware of the importance

of this decision and their part in it, from aged 16 to
106. The turnout far exceeded normal elections, and
Scotland has been changed regardless of the
immediate outcome. The Democracy Trail points
forward but Scotland's citizens have already
travelled a long and remarkable road to reach this
point in time. Understanding where we have come
from is always helpful in deciding where we should
go next.

From Holyrood you can look back to Calton Hill
and its unique combination of war memorials and

▲ Yes Rally at the Scottish Parliament
    Courtesy of Danielle Watt

monuments to democracy and progressive thought. Modern Scotland was shaped by Empire, industrialisation, World War and emigration. Yet its own democratic voices have never been silenced through the maelstrom of change, and Holyrood unites the ancient traditions of Scotland's Commonweal with the present and the future.

On Calton Hill, looking out over the Forth, protesters often sang Hamish Henderson's international anthem, 'Freedom Come-All-Ye', which was originally written for the ant-nuclear peace marchers at the Holy Loch in 1961, and seems to sum up the radical vision.

> Roch the wind in the clear day's dawin
> Blaws the cloods heilster-gowdie ow'r the bay
> But there's mair nor a roch wind blawin
> Thro the Great Glen o the warld the day
> It's a thocht that wad gar oor rottans
> Aa thae rogues that gang gallus fresh an gay
> Tak the road an seek ither loanins
> Wi thair ill ploys tae sport an play
>
> Nae mair will our bonnie callants
> Merch tae war when oor braggarts crousely craw
> Nor wee weans frae pitheid an clachan
> Mourn the ships sailin doun the Broomielaw
> Broken faimlies in lands we've hairriet
> Will curse 'Scotland the Brave' nae mair, nae mair;
> Black an white ane-til-ither mairriet
> Mak the vile barracks o thair maisters bare
>
> Sae come aa ye at hame wi freedom
> Never heed whit the houdies croak for Doom
> In yer hoose aa the bairns o Adam
> Will find breid, barley-bree an paintit room
> When Maclean meets wi's friens in Springburn
> Aa thae roses an geans will turn tae blume,
> An yon black boy frae yont Nyanga
> Dings the fell gallows o the burghers doun.

When the Holyrood building opened in 2004, Sheena Wellington brought the ceremonial to a moment of spine tingling unity with Robert Burns' defining statement of human equality and worth, 'A Man's A Man For Aa That'.

> Is there for honest Poverty
> That hings his head, an aa that;
> The coward slave – we pass him by,
> We daur be poor for aa that!
> For aw that, an aa that.
> Our toils obscure an aa that,
> The rank is but the guinea's stamp,
> The Man's the gowd for aa that.

▲ The Political Martyrs' Monument, Old Calton Cemetery

What though on hamely fare we dine,
Wear hodden grey, an aa that;
Gie fools their silks, and knaves their wine;
A Man's a Man for aa that:
For aw that, and aa that,
Their tinsel show, an aa that;
The honest man, tho e'ersae poor,
Is king o men for aa that.

Ye see yon birkie, caw'd a lord,
Wha struts, an stares, an aa that;
Tho hundreds worship at his word,
He's but a coof for aa that:
For aw that, an aa that,
His ribband, star, an aa that:
The man o independent mind
He looks an laughs at aa that.

A prince can mak a belted knight,
A marquis, duke, an aa that;
Butan honest mans aboon his might,
Gude faith, he maunnafaa that!
For aa that, an aa that,
Their dignities an aa that;
The pith o sense, an pride o worth,
Are higher rank than aa that.

Then let us pray that come it may,
(As come it will for aa that),
That Sense and Worth, o'er aa the earth,
Shall bear the gree, an aa that.
For aw that, an aa that,
It's coming yet for aa that,
That Man to Man, the world o'er,
Shall brothers be for aa that.

Timeline

16th Century: Humanist Scholars and Reformers, Protestant and Catholic Reformations

John Mair (1467–1550)

George Buchanan (1506–1582)

1552	The poet David Lyndsay's coruscating *Ane Satyre of the Thrie Estaitis* was first performed in Edinburgh. Although attacking all three 'Estaitis' – the Clergy, Government and Commerce – this bawdy and hugely entertaining work, five hours long in its full version, targeted in particular the corruption of the clergy.
1559–1561	The Scottish Reformation. Responding to European ideas and local corruption as exposed by Lyndsay the Reformation overthrew Catholicism and introduced Presbyterianism into Scotland. It also allowed the nobility to acquire all the lands of the Catholic Church.

17th Century: Renaissance, Early Enlightenment and the Wars of Religion

1603	The Union of the Crowns
1638	The National Covenant signed throughout Scotland calling for resistance against the imposition of essentially English religious practices

by Charles I and Archbishop William Laud.

1639–1651   The Wars of the Three Kingdoms. The religious and political disputes in Scotland, England and Ireland caused by Charles I's insistence on his right to dictate not only public policy but also the people's choice of religion. This led to the formation of the Commonwealth under Lord Protector Oliver Cromwell and horrific indiscriminate slaughters in Drogheda and Dundee.

1660   The Restoration of the Stuart Monarchy sees Charles II ushered in. Further religious and political turmoil ensues.

1689   James VII and II is overthrown by the English Parliament and William of Orange installed as King.

18th Century: Enlightenment, European Empires, American Independence and French Revolution

1707   Union of the Scottish and English Parliaments resulted in widespread rioting throughout Scotland.

1708   Failed attempt at invasion of Scotland by exiled James VII.

1715   Jacobite Rising led disastrously by 'Bobbing John', the Earl of Mar, one of Queen Anne's Commissioners in the lead up to the Union.

1719	Battle of Glen Shiel. Pathetic Jacobite rising in the North West.
1729	Francis Hutcheson becomes Chair of Moral Philosophy at Glasgow University. His work can be considered a precursor to the Scottish Enlightenment.
1745–1746	Further unsuccessful Jacobite Rising led by the charismatic Prince Charles Edward Stuart, otherwise known as Bonnie Prince Charlie. After defeat at Culloden, sporadic guerrilla campaigning continues until early 1750s.
1750s	Growth of Scottish Enlightenment in Edinburgh and Glasgow.
1759	Birth of Robert Burns. Final defeat of Prince Charles at naval battle of Quiberon Bay.
1760s	Enlightenment ideas spread.
1790s	Scottish Radicalism inspired by writings of Thomas Paine and French and American Revolutions.
1792	The convention of the Societies of the Friends of the People meets in Edinburgh 11 December. 'Year of the Sheep' in Sutherland as Highland Clearances gather pace.
1793	Show trials of Scottish Martyrs and others for sedition. Vicious clampdown on dissent.

19th Century: Napoleonic Wars, Industrialisation, the Expansion of British Empire and the Extension of the Franchise

1800 onwards	The expansion of British Empire continues with continual use of Scottish regiments as frontline troops.
1809	Further mass clearances of population in Sutherland by notorious Patrick Sellar.
1819	Massacre of Peterloo in Manchester. Dragoons attack Reformist crowd.
1820	Scottish rising led by weavers, heavily manipulated by *agents provocateurs*. So-called leaders Baird and Hardie executed for treason.
1832–1834	Passage of Parliamentary Reform Acts ending in blatant corruption of parliament and extending franchise.
1843	The 'Disruption' as Presbyterian Church splits.
1846	Widespread famine in rural areas due to potato blight increases already established patterns of emigration.
1848	Chartist riots demanding further electoral reform.
1856	Agitation for eight-hour day causes riots in the West.
1859	First miners' strike.
1870 onwards	Development of Irish Home Rule movement influences Scottish Land Reformers.

1872	Education (Scotland) Act promotes universal education but bans the indigenous languages of Gaelic and Scots from the classroom.
1880	Formation of the Highland Land League to address problems of land use and clearances.
1882	Battle of the Braes on Skye as crofters fight police brought in to serve eviction notices.
1883	Napier Commission formed to investigate land problems.
1893	Keir Hardie elected as first Socialist MP.
1897	Congested District Board set up to help crofters.

20th Century: The First World War, Irish Independence, The Great Depression and the Second World War

1908	Glendale Skye first community ownership of land.
1909	Formation of Second Highland Land League (HLL) as a political party.
1918	HLL affiliates with Labour Party.
1948	Knoydart land raid unsuccessful
1949	The Scottish Covenant. Two million Scots sign this petition for Home Rule. This was ignored by Westminster.
1955	Crofters Act and Founding of Crofters Commission.

1976	Crofting right to buy established.
1979	Yes vote for a Scottish Assembly vetoed by Labour MP amendment demanding 40 per cent of the electorate must support it. First past the post remains the rule for Westminster. Margaret Thatcher's Conservative government comes to power.
1983	The Conservative Party wins another overall majority at Westminster despite only drawing 28 per cent of the vote in Scotland.
1988	Margaret Thatcher delivers her much criticised 'Sermon on the Mound' to the General Assembly of the Church of Scotland in May, in which she offered a theological defence of capitalism and deregulation.
1989	Thatcher's government trials the deeply unpopular Poll Tax in Scotland, before introducing it in England and Wales the following year.
1992	Conservatives win general election with only 25 per cent of the vote in Scotland. Vigil for a Scottish Parliament founded.
1993	Assynt Estate becomes community owned.
1997	Conservatives wiped out in Scotland, Labour's election win ensures Scottish devolution.

| 1997 | Island of Eigg community buy-out. |
| 1999 | First election of the Scottish Parliament. |

21st Century: The Rise of China and India, the Clash of Cultures and Financial Crisis in the West

2003	Labour majority in the second Scottish General Election.
2004	Opening of Holyrood Parliament.
2007	SNP form minority government at Holyrood.
2010	Crofting Reform (Scotland) Act.
2011	SNP overall majority in Scottish General Election.
2014	Independence Referendum.

Some other books published by **LUATH** PRESS

Calton Hill: Journeys and Evocations

Stuart McHardy and Donald Smith

ISBN: 978-1-908373-85-4 PBK

£7.99

Experience the scenery and folklore of Edinburgh's iconic Calton Hill through new eyes in the second instalment in McHardy and Smith's Journeys and Evocations series. This blend of prose, poetry, photography and history is the perfect gift for any visitor to Scotland's capital city.

McHardy is driven by a passion for making connections. His vision is of an interconnected, inter-related environment. His values are those of a cultural ecologist, storyteller as well as researcher, poet as well as scholar. He sets out to illuminate and to persuade.
CENCRASTUS

Arthur's Seat: Journeys and Evocations

Stuart McHardy and Donald Smith

ISBN: 978-1-908373-46-5 PBK

£7.99

Arthur's Seat, rising high above the Edinburgh skyline, is the city's most awe-inspiring landmark. Although thousands climb to the summit every year, its history remains a mystery, shrouded in myth and legend.

The first book of its kind, *Arthur's Seat: Journeys and Evocations* is a salute to the ancient tradition of storytelling, guiding the reader around Edinburgh's famous 'Resting Giant' with an exploration of the local folklore and customs associated with the mountain-within-a-city.

Inspired by NVA's Speed of Light, a major event in Edinburgh's International Festival and the country-wide Cultural Olympiad, *Journeys and Evocations* brings together past and future in a perspective of the Edinburgh landscape like no other.

Edinburgh Old Town

John Fee, with Stuart McHardy
and Donald Smith
ISBN: 978-1-910021-56-9 PBK
£7.99

 *John Fee was a true storytelling artist, painting verbal pictures, setting off on digressions that turned out not to be digressions, moving effortlessly into a song or poem. He has uncovered little-known aspects of the Royal Mile along with long-forgotten characters who spring back to life through the storyteller's art.*

Following on from the acclaimed *Arthur's Seat* and *Calton Hill* volumes, this third instalment in the Journeys and Evocations series focuses on the extensive history and folklore surrounding Edinburgh's atmospheric Old Town. Take a vivid trip with John Fee through Edinburgh's Old Town as you've never seen it before, with this wonderful blend of prose, poetry, photography and incredible stories from another era of one of Edinburgh's most renowned districts.

Let's Explore Edinburgh Old Town

Anne Bruce English
Illustrations by Cinders McLeod
ISBN: 978-0-946487-98-1 PBK
£4.99

 The Old Town of Edinburgh has everything. At the highest point is a huge castle. At the foot of the hill there's a palace.

Between them are secret gardens, a museum full of toys, a statue of the world famous Greyfriars Bobby, and much more besides.

There were murders here too (think of Burke and Hare). There's mystery – is preacher John Knox really buried under parking space 44? And then there are the ghosts of Mary King's Close.

You can find out about all this and more in this guide. Read the tales of the Old Town, check out the short quizzes and the Twenty Questions page (all the answers are given), and you'll have plenty to see and do. Join Anne and Cinders on a fascinating and fun journey through time.

Details of these and other books published by Luath Press can be found at: **www.luath.co.uk**

Luath Press Limited

committed to publishing well written books worth reading

LUATH PRESS takes its name from Robert Burns, whose little collie Luath (*Gael.*, swift or nimble) tripped up Jean Armour at a wedding and gave him the chance to speak to the woman who was to be his wife and the abiding love of his life.

Burns called one of 'The Twa Dogs' Luath after Cuchullin's hunting dog in Ossian's *Fingal*. Luath Press was established in 1981 in the heart of Burns country, and now resides a few steps up the road from Burns' first lodgings on Edinburgh's Royal Mile.

Luath offers you distinctive writing with a hint of unexpected pleasures.

Most bookshops in the UK, the US, Canada, Australia, New Zealand and parts of Europe either carry our books in stock or can order them for you. To order direct from us, please send a £sterling cheque, postal order, international money order or your credit card details (number, address of cardholder and expiry date) to us at the address below. Please add post and packing as follows: UK – £1.00 per delivery address; overseas surface mail – £2.50 per delivery address; overseas airmail – £3.50 for the first book to each delivery address, plus £1.00 for each additional book by airmail to the same address. If your order is a gift, we will happily enclose your card or message at no extra charge.

Luath Press Limited
543/2 Castlehill
The Royal Mile
Edinburgh EH1 2ND
Scotland
Telephone: 0131 225 4326 (24 hours)
email: sales@luath.co.uk
Website: www.luath.co.uk